❇ Your Exclusive

As a sign of our endless gratitude, we have prepared a special gift just for you. Not only will you have access to your current copy of the book in an exclusive digital color edition, further enriching your visual and culinary experience, but we've also reserved an additional gift for you.

"THE SUPERFOOD CODE: Explore Time-Tested Foods and Empower Your Health" is your extra ticket to a food discovery adventure, offering you a deep dive into the superfoods that have nourished and enriched generations, thanks to the secrets and practices revealed in the book.

🔥 Your Grilling Adventure Begins NOW! 🔥

Your culinary journey with us is just heating up! In addition to your exclusive bonuses, we're thrilled to also present you with a sizzling surprise: "THE PIT BOSS COOKBOOK"! Get ready to uplift your grilling skills, surprise your loved ones with newfound culinary prowess, and embark on countless food adventures with the trusty Pit Boss by your side. Unlock secrets to crafting mouthwatering dishes that will not only satisfy your taste buds but also ignite a flame of excitement in every bite.

Get your Bonuses in the last chapter!

THE CARNIVORE CODE

Cookbook for Beginners

Unlock Ancestral Health by Meat-Power Boost.

14-Day Carnivore Diet Reset | Bonus

Michelle Burns

CONTENTS

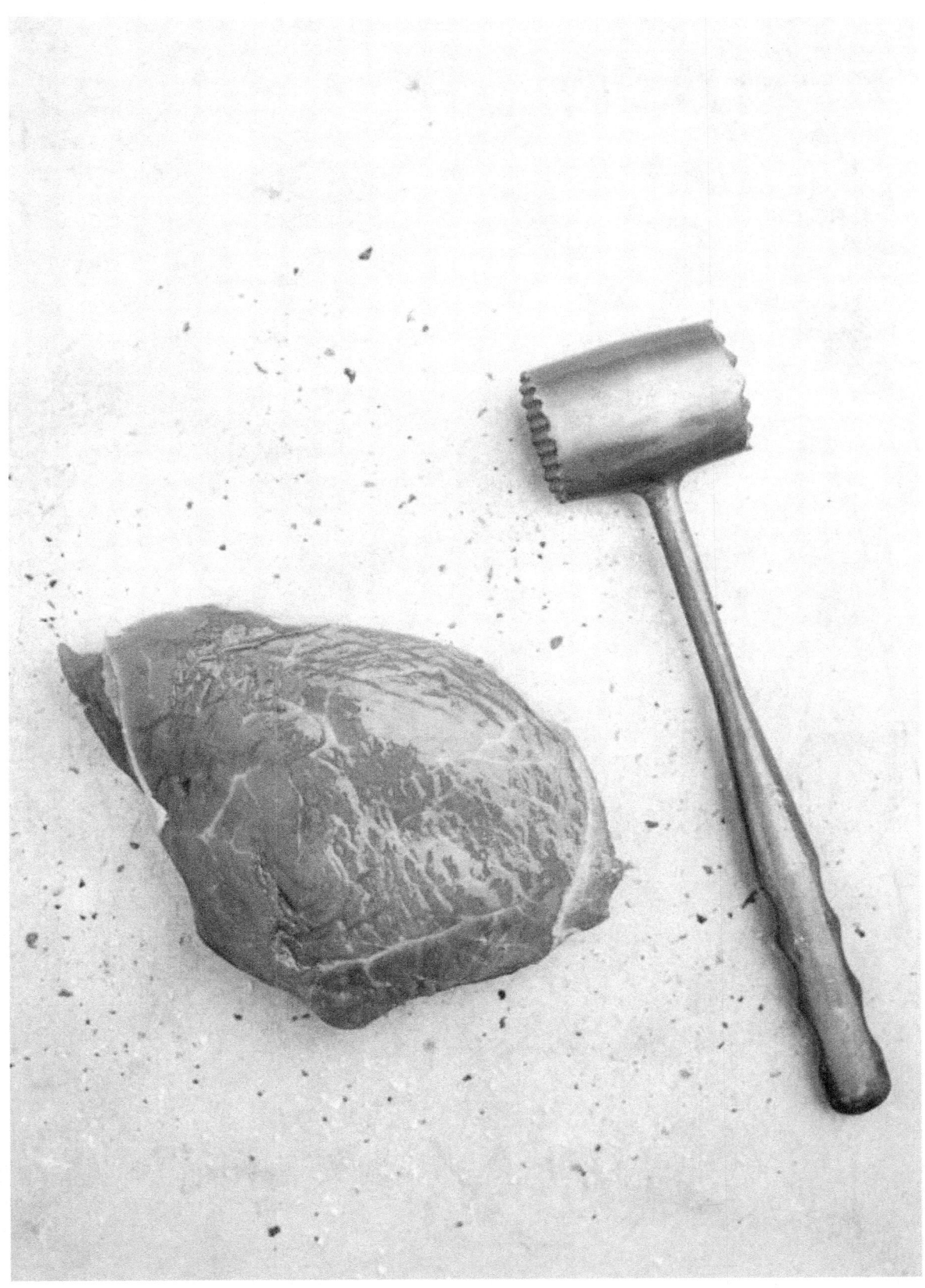

THE CARNIVORE DIET

History and evolution

At first look, the carnivore diet may appear to be a modern or even innovative approach to nutrition. Its essence, however, is firmly established in our evolutionary history, harkening back to a time when our early human ancestors relied mostly on animal products for nutrition. Meat, especially from large game, was a cherished and crucial food source for these early humans, who were hunter-gatherers by nature. The exact percentage of plant-to-animal food they ingested is a point of contention among historians and anthropologists, but the importance of meat in their diet cannot be overstated.

This dietary emphasis began to alter some 10,000 years ago, with the onset of the Agricultural Revolution. Humans began to cultivate crops when they transitioned from nomadic lifestyles to stable societies, resulting in a large increase in plant-based meals in their diet. Grains, legumes, and, subsequently, dairy products evolved as new staples, gradually pushing animal-based meals to the margins.

Fast forward to the twentieth and twenty-first centuries, and we see even more dramatic changes in nutritional trends. Processed meals, refined sugars, and an onslaught of artificial substances began to dominate the global food landscape. This modern nutritional paradigm, combined with more sedentary lives, has resulted in an alarming increase in chronic diseases, obesity, and metabolic disorders.

Many dietary movements with a range of remedies have emerged in reaction to these health concerns. The re-emerging carnivore diet was one of them. This diet advocated a return to a traditional nutritional philosophy by focusing solely on the consumption of animal products. Its potential to treat a wide range of health problems, including autoimmune disorders and inflammation, was highlighted by supporters. The carnivore diet has, however, seen its fair share of skepticism and criticism, as with any dietary movement that goes against the grain. Potential nutrient imbalances, sustainability over the long run, and other health issues have all been raised as concerns.

As we go further into "The Carnivore Code Bible Cookbook for Beginners," we'll not only break down the basic tenets of the carnivore diet but also show you how to use them in real life to make nourishing and enticing meals. Whether you approach this book with a healthy dose of skepticism or a firm devotion to the carnivore way of life, it promises insights and gastronomic delights to elevate your nutritional inquiry.

Benefits of the Carnivore Diet

- **Simplicity:** Meal preparation and planning might be simple if there is no need to select from a wide variety of food types. This ease of use can make cooking and grocery shopping less intimidating for some people.

- **Potential Therapeutic Effects:** Anecdotal data indicates that the carnivore diet may be effective in treating several medical issues, including autoimmune illnesses, inflammation, and even mood disorders.

- **Nutrient Density:** Omega-3 fatty acids, complete proteins, Iron, B vitamins, and zinc are among the necessary nutrients that animal products are rich in. Compared to supplies from plants, they frequently provide these nutrients in ways that are more accessible.

- **Digestive Health:** The intestinal health of many persons following a carnivorous diet has improved. By avoiding plant-based foods, individuals can stay away from potential irritants and anti-nutrients like lectins and phytic acid.

Challenges for Beginners

- **Nutritional Concerns:** The risk of omitting important nutrients like fiber, certain vitamins, and minerals that are largely present in plant meals exists if proper planning is not made.

- **Transition Symptoms:** Some people may notice signs like exhaustion, headaches, or digestive issues when their bodies get used to a diet that exclusively contains meat. As the body adjusts, these symptoms — often referred to as "carnivore flu" — normally get better.

- **Limited Variety:** Meals can get repetitive over time if you only eat things that come from animals. It can be difficult to keep people interested if you don't find creative ways to prepare meat.
- **Social Implications:** It can be difficult to eat out or participate in social events. Traditional foods and recipes are not often carnivore-friendly.
- **Sustainability and Ethical Concerns:** A diet high in meat is said to have negative environmental effects. For individuals who care about animal welfare and the environment, buying meat that has been ethically raised and sustainably harvested can be more expensive.

Choosing to follow a carnivorous diet is a journey that you must take for yourself, one that is strewn with both opportunities for improvement and real obstacles. Even if there are many possible benefits, it's crucial for newcomers to be aware of any potential obstacles and have a plan in place on how to overcome them. Whether you are interested in the carnivore diet for health benefits or just out of curiosity, having a thorough understanding of it will help you succeed.

Basic principles and tenets

- **Listen to Your Body:** The impact of a carnivorous diet can differ from person to person. Even though many people report more energy and better health indicators, it's important to pay attention to your body's signals. Consider speaking with a nutritionist or healthcare provider if your unpleasant symptoms persist for a long time.
- **Prioritize Animal Foods:** The carnivore diet is fundamentally focused on eating items with animal origins. This comprises animal products such as meat (beef, pork, poultry, and fish), organs (liver, kidneys, and heart), eggs, and occasionally dairy. In many interpretations, these foods are the only items allowed in the diet, not only the focal point.
- **Be Mindful of Food Quality:** Quality must always come first, especially with the focus on animal meals. Meats from animals that have been caught in the wild, fed grass, or grown on pasture are preferred. In addition to being free of dangerous chemicals and hormones, these sources frequently contain higher concentrations of advantageous nutrients like omega-3 fatty acids.

- **Embrace Nose-to-Tail Eating:** The "nose-to-tail" approach to eating is frequently encouraged by the carnivore diet rather than merely eating muscular meats. Using the entire animal, including its organs and bone marrow, is what this means. This strategy offers a wider range of nutrients while also reducing waste. Particularly rich in nutrients and able to supply large quantities of vitamins and minerals, organ meats are a great source of these nutrients.

- **Limit or Eliminate Plant Foods:** The strictest interpretations of the carnivore diet forbid any plant items, but certain varieties might allow for a small amount of plant ingestion (such as herbs for seasoning or occasionally low-carb veggies). To prevent potential irritants, allergies, and anti-nutrients that may be contained in some plant foods.

- **Stay Hydrated, But Limit Plant-Based Drinks:** The carnivorous diet is no different when it comes to the importance of water. The majority of teas, coffees, and practically all alcoholic beverages come from plants, yet these are usually prohibited or restricted.

Although the fundamentals of the carnivore diet are simple, they can differ significantly from the typical Western diet. Adopting these ideas calls for dedication and frequently involves some amount of adjustment. But the rewards can be significant for those who find accord with its ideals. It is always a good idea to begin with awareness, attention, and care because individual experiences may differ as with any nutritional plan.

Science behind a meat-based diet: Benefits, myths, and controversies

In recent years, the carnivore, or meat-based, diet has become more and more popular, drawing support from both supporters and detractors. This diet is based on the premise that animal products are our primary source of nutrition because of the way our bodies are built. Let's go more deeply into the research underlying this strategy, examining the alleged advantages, dispelling common misconceptions, and emphasizing the current debates.

The high nutritional density of meat is one of the main advantages associated with it. Complete proteins, B vitamins, iron, zinc, and omega-3 fatty acids are just a few of the important nutrients that animal products are high in. These nutrients are frequently found in human-bioavailable forms. In contrast to non-heme iron from plant sources, heme iron from meat is more easily absorbed. Additionally, the proper ratios of necessary amino acids found in meats are crucial for the synthesis of muscle and metabolic health in general. Supporters of the carnivore diet frequently highlight potential medicinal advantages in addition to nutritional value. The effectiveness of the diet in treating autoimmune illnesses, chronic inflammation, and some neurological conditions is suggested by anecdotal reports and recent studies.

By avoiding plant-based foods, one might avoid potential allergens and antinutrients including lectins, oxalates, and phytic acid, which some theories claim can increase gut permeability and trigger inflammatory reactions. A discussion of a meat-based diet, however, would be incomplete without debunking common misconceptions.

One of these myths is the idea that eating a certain way will result in high cholesterol and raise your risk of developing heart disease. Modern research indicates that eating cholesterol has no effect on blood cholesterol for the majority of people, even though meat, especially red meat, contains cholesterol and saturated fats. A few studies suggest that saturated fats may not be as bad for heart health as previously thought, which is another way the story surrounding them is changing.

Another myth is the idea that consuming too much protein would damage the kidneys. For healthy people, there is minimal evidence to suggest that a high-protein diet has negative effects on kidney function, while those with pre-existing renal problems are advised to watch protein intake.

Several debates continue despite the advantages and myth-busting. Dietary fiber, which is mostly obtained from plant foods and is known to support gut health and facilitate digestion, is one key issue. Critics also draw attention to the potential dangers of omitting phytonutrients, antioxidants, and certain vitamins that are only present in plants and have a role in reducing oxidative stress and enhancing general health.

And last, a major source of debate continues to be the ethical and environmental effects of a diet that emphasizes meat. Because raising animals requires a lot of resources, critics claim that eating this way could make environmental issues worse. Some people support meats that are properly sourced and that have been reared humanely because of ethical concerns about animal welfare.

Finally, the carnivore diet, based on current nutritional knowledge and evolutionary biology, makes a strong case for a healthful diet that emphasizes meat. It is not a one-size-fits-all diet though, just like all other diets. Individual tastes, ethical considerations, and health requirements will always be at the forefront of dietary decisions as science develops and we continue to clarify our understanding. Whether one chooses a meat-based diet or another dietary strategy, making well-informed decisions that are supported by science and reflection is still crucial.

RULES & SECRETS

One may feel as like they are entering unfamiliar territory while transitioning to a carnivore diet, especially if they have grown up with a varied or typical Western diet. More than just changing the way you eat is needed for the transformation; you also need to adjust your body and change your thinking, as well as develop a sustainable plan. The transition from a varied diet to one that emphasizes meat is examined in more detail here.

Understanding the driving forces behind your choice is crucial before starting this journey. Are your motivations primarily related to your physical performance, your general interest, or your concerns about your health? When difficulties arise, being able to identify your reasons can be a help. Whether the end goals are symptom relief, increased energy, or enhanced overall well-being, it serves as a reminder of what's important in the long run.

It can be exhausting physically and mentally to suddenly change one's diet. Consider a progressive approach as opposed to an abrupt change. As you gradually cut back on plant-based diets, start by consuming more animal items. The process can be made more manageable and less daunting by this gradual adjustment. Furthermore, it provides your body time to adapt to the new food sources, thus reducing stomach issues or "carnivore flu" symptoms.

To make sure you're still having all necessary nutrients you require when you transition to meat-focused plan, it's crucial. Even though animal products are nutrient-dense, you can first lose out on several substances that are generally found in plants. Consider adding supplements like vitamin C or magnesium in the beginning, if necessary. You might discover that you need fewer vitamins as time goes on when you adopt "nose-to-tail" eating and broaden your meat intake.

When you're not struggling through change alone, it's always easier. To meet seasoned carnivores, look for local or online networks, forums, or groups. Making the journey more pleasurable and educational can be accomplished by exchanging stories, recipes, and challenges with like-minded people.

The best indicator of any nutritional change is your body, which cannot be emphasized enough. Be mindful of your feelings while you make the change. Feedback on your mood, digestion, sleep patterns, and energy levels is all important. Consider changing your strategy, getting advice from a nutritionist, or even reintroducing some foods to see what happens if something feels weird. Following a varied dietary history, switching to a carnivore diet is a significant change that can have positive effects but also calls for commitment and adaptability. Everybody will have a different experience because it is a personal journey. The most essential thing is to enjoy the culinary journey of finding the primordial essence of food. Arm yourself with information, be patient, and do all three.

In particular, when examined through the perspective of current dietary thinking, the idea that humans may fulfill all of our nutritional demands through meat alone can seem contradictory. But when we go more into the rich tapestry of human evolutionary history and nutritional science, the concept of a meat-centric diet starts to tell a tale that is both fascinating and irresistible. Historically, numerous indigenous civilizations have flourished on diets that were mostly reliant on animal products, including the Maasai in Africa and the Inuit in the Arctic. The fact that these civilizations not only survived but frequently displayed amazing health and energy, suggests that meat can be a crucial component of human nutrition. But to grasp this, we must challenge some long-held dietary assumptions.

Its excellent macronutrient profile is at the core of meat's superior nutritional qualities. All nine of the essential amino acids are present in enough amounts within animal products, ensuring that they are of the highest quality for human consumption. The building blocks of our muscles, enzymes, hormones, and a variety of other vital physiological processes, amino acids are essential for human health.

But proteins aren't the only factor. A balance between omega-3 and omega-6 fatty acids can be found in animal fats, especially those from pasture-raised or wild-caught sources. Contrary to long-held misconceptions, lipids are essential for maintaining healthy cells, supporting brain function, and allowing the body to absorb fat-soluble vitamins like A, D, E, and K. These necessary fats are found in meat in forms that our bodies recognize and can effectively utilize, especially when it comes from animals that have been grown in their natural environments and fed on their native diets.

In addition to macronutrients, meat's micronutrient profile further supports its nutritional merits. Organ meats are a important providers of vitamins and minerals and are frequently called "nature's multivitamins." For instance, the liver is a powerhouse of vitamin B12, iron, choline, and vitamin A, whereas the heart provides an abundance of coenzyme Q10, which is crucial for cellular energy production. We are guaranteed to fulfill, if not frequently surpass, our nutritional needs thanks to these organ meats.

However, the subject of what happens to fiber, anti-oxidants, and other phytonutrients that are found only in plants frequently comes up. The carnivore story takes an intriguing turn at this point. The body's ability to adapt to an environment rich in meat and the decreased stomach irritation caused by the absence of plant-based anti-nutrients are two arguments made by supporters of the idea that the human requirement for fiber is greatly exaggerated. It is argued that the body's requirement for antioxidants and phytonutrients decreases in the absence of irritants derived from high carbohydrate and plant-based diets.

There are limitations, though, as there always are with significant dietary changes. Nutrient imbalances could result from a diet that only includes muscular meat. It is essential to have a holistic strategy that incorporates consumption from nose to tail. This guarantees a variety of nutrients, including collagen in tendons and a wide range of minerals in the bone marrow.

Finally, the notion that eating meat can complete one's nutritional needs is more than just a trend in terms of eating habits. It is evidence of the human body's evolutionary development and flexibility. It might not be the best option for everyone, but for those who take this route, the secret is to learn the subtleties, find high-quality meats, and enjoy the hearty, primitive flavors that have supported our forebears for millennia.

Common misconceptions and pitfalls

When navigating the carnivorous diet, there are many misunderstandings, partial truths, and dangers to watch out for. It's critical to distinguish fact from fiction and take proactive measures to address common issues to fully accept and benefit from this nutritional strategy.

Misconception: "Meat Causes Heart Disease and High Cholesterol"

Older dietary recommendations that linked dietary cholesterol and saturated fats to heart disease are where this notion first emerged. A more nuanced picture is painted, nonetheless, by more recent research. Saturated fats can increase LDL cholesterol, or "bad cholesterol," but they also frequently increase HDL, or "good cholesterol." Furthermore, research has found that cholesterol present in diet does not influence blood cholesterol in most individuals. Inflammation, triglyceride levels, and LDL particle size all play significant roles in the complex picture of heart health. Make decisions based on current research, and seek advice from medical professionals.

Pitfall: Solely Relying on Muscle Meats

Consuming only muscle foods, such as steaks and chicken breasts, is a mistake beginners frequently make. Although they are delectable, they do not provide the same range of nutrients that an animal would. Unbalanced nutrient intake might result from skipping organ meats, bone broth, and other animal parts. Adopting a "nose to tail" philosophy ensures a more comprehensive intake of nutrients, from the iron in the liver to the collagen in animal tendons.

Misconception: "You'll Get Scurvy without Vitamin C from Plants"

When talking about the carnivore diet, a common worry is scurvy, a condition brought on by a vitamin C deficit. Scurvy has always been a problem for sailors on long trips since fresh produce was scarce. A low-carb or ketogenic diet, however, dramatically reduces the body's need for vitamin C, which is less well-known. The small levels of vitamin C found in organ meats, particularly the liver, may be sufficient given the reduced need for a diet heavy on meat.

Pitfall: Not Being Prepared for Social Situations

Given its unique approach, the carnivore diet might offer difficulties at social gatherings like dinners, parties, or eating out. Without planning, it's simple to stray from the diet or have difficult talks. It is advantageous to prepare ahead of time; you can do this by eating beforehand, calling restaurants to ask about meat-only menu alternatives, or even bringing your food to shared meals. These circumstances grow easier to navigate with experience.

Misconception: "A Meat-Only Diet is Monotonous"

Many people refer to variety as the flavor of life, and detractors claim that the diet of a carnivore lacks this. Animal products have a huge and diverse market. The carnivore diet can be as varied and savory as any other diet, with a wide variety of meat cuts, fish varieties, and organ meats as well as a variety of cooking techniques, including grilling, roasting, stewing, or even eating food raw like sashimi or tartare.

It's crucial to approach the carnivore diet with an open mind, supported by extensive knowledge and personal experience, in the constantly changing world of nutrition. By dispelling myths and avoiding typical mistakes, one can not only travel this journey more easily but also enjoy all the flavors and numerous advantages that this distinctive dietary path has to offer.

NUTRITIONAL COMPLETENESS & COOKING TECHNIQUES

Meat is a wide-ranging and diverse food. Each kind of meat has a distinct nutrient profile, whether it comes from terrestrial animals or marine life. Individuals who consume a lot of or just animal products may benefit from optimizing their nutritional intake by understanding these characteristics. Let's investigate various meats' nutritional profiles.

Beef (Red Meat):

- Protein: A prime provider of protein having all required amino acids.
- B Vitamins: Especially rich in B12, crucial for nerve function and the formation of red blood cells.
- Minerals: Notably high in zinc, selenium, iron (more bioavailable heme iron), and phosphorus.
- Fats: Contains saturated fats, monounsaturated fats, and omega-6 and omega-3 fatty acids, especially if grass-fed.

Chicken (Poultry):

- Protein: Another great source of complete protein.
- B Vitamins: Rich in niacin (B3) which aids in metabolism, and B6, essential for brain health.
- Minerals: Good source of selenium, phosphorus, and zinc.
- Fats: Leaner cuts like chicken breast are lower in fat, while thighs and wings have higher fat content.

Fish (Aquatic Meat):

- Protein: Fish provide high-quality protein, though the content may vary between species.
- Omega-3 Fats: Fish like sardines, salmon, and mackerel are rich in EPA and DHA, crucial for brain and heart health.
- Vitamins: Vitamin D is abundant in fatty fish. Also, fish are a unique source of iodine.
- Minerals: High in selenium, phosphorus, and potassium.

Pork:

- Protein: Offers complete protein, akin to beef.
- B Vitamins: Particularly high in thiamin (B1), which plays a vital role in energy production.
- Minerals: Good source of selenium, zinc, and phosphorus.
- Fats: Contains saturated and monounsaturated fats.

Organ Meats (Offal):

- Liver: A true nutrient powerhouse. Exceptionally high in vitamin A, copper, and B vitamins, especially B12 and folate.
- Heart: Rich in coenzyme Q10, essential for energy production in cells.
- Kidneys: Good source of B12, riboflavin (B2), and iron.
- Brain: Contains omega-3 fatty acids and cholesterol, vital for brain health.

The larger context must be understood even though this breakdown provides a look into the nutritional diversity of meats. Depending on an animal's diet, age, and Instructions of preparation and cooking, the meat's nutrient composition can change. In comparison to grain-fed beef, grass-fed beef often has a greater omega-3 concentration. Similar to this, the nutritional profile of wild-caught fish differs from that of farmed fish. Diversification is essential for maximizing nutritional absorption on a diet heavy on meat. A balanced and comprehensive nutrient intake can be achieved by alternating between different meats and including both muscle and organ meats. A carnivore's journey may be both nourishing and enjoyable thanks to the variety that not only meets our bodies' needs but also adds a mix of flavors and textures to the dish.

The role of organ meats in a balanced carnivore diet

While roast chicken and steaks have an unmistakable draw for carnivores, there is an unsung hero who deserves at least as much attention: organ meats, or "offal." Organ meats have long been considered a gastronomic treat and a nutritional powerhouse, offering a variety of nutrients that are either in short supply or missing from regular muscle meats. They have long been cherished across civilizations.

Organ meats are highly nutrient-dense and are frequently referred to as nature's multivitamins. Let's say you're eating beef liver. Vitamin A, essential for vision, immune system health, and cellular health in general, is stored in this single organ. However, its nutritional generosity doesn't end there; it is also abundant in necessary minerals e.g. copper and iron, and a range of B vitamins, which provide appropriate energy metabolism and neuron function. In the liver, choline is also present in greater concentrations than in other food sources, making it essential for metabolism, liver function, and brain health.

But other organ meats besides simply liver are also healthy. Heart health and cellular energy are supported by the heart's high CoQ10 content. As opposed to this, the kidneys offer a special combination of selenium and B12. The brain is another source of essential fatty acids that, despite being less popular, are vital for cognitive function.

In a healthy carnivore diet, organ meats also serve a crucial role in sustainability, in addition to their nutritional value. A nose-to-tail strategy honors the life of the animal by utilizing all that it has to offer while ensuring that more of the animal is used and less waste is produced. This philosophy is in line with our predecessors' customs, who instinctively understood the benefits of eating the complete animal. It also accords with the ecological ideals of sustainability.

Including organ meats in your diet is crucial for anyone adopting or already living a carnivorous lifestyle. Assuring a holistic nutrient intake is just as important as mixing up one's plate. While some people may find the flavor or texture of offal unfamiliar, with the proper preparation and an open mind, these organ meats can change from unsettling anomalies into beloved staples that nourish the body and enhance the carnivorous experience.

Addressing Concerns: Vitamins, Minerals, and Other Essential Nutrients on a Carnivore Diet

When one enters the world of carnivores, there are frequently a lot of things to worry about, particularly when one considers the range of nutrients we have been taught to get from plants. The concerns are numerous, ranging from the powerful vitamin C in citrus fruits to the healthy fibers in grains. However, a thorough examination of the nutritional composition of animal products yields startling revelations that contradict conventional dietary notions.

The Vitamin Spectrum: A juicy orange or a piece of kiwi can come to mind when one thinks of vitamin C. The catch is that although this vitamin is abundant in plant sources, the carnivorous diet lowers the body's need for it. The cause? The body needs less vitamin C when it consumes fewer carbohydrates. Additionally, organ meats, especially the liver, provide modest but enough levels of Vitamin C to guard against deficits.

Vitamin B12 is another necessary component that plays a crucial role in blood and nerve production. Unlike animal goods, which are rich in B12, plant diets are free of it. Organ meats and shellfish are particularly high in B12. Similar to this, fatty fish like salmon and mackerel are a great source of vitamin D, that supports the immunity and bone health.

Mineral Mastery: Animal products are abundant in minerals, which are unheralded heroes of our metabolic processes. The movement of oxygen in our blood, for instance, depends on iron. Compared to non-heme iron from plant sources, heme iron from meat, particularly red meat, is more effectively absorbed by our bodies. Another mineral abundantly present in meat is zinc, which is crucial for immune system health and wound healing. Oysters have the greatest zinc level of any food. Then there is calcium, which is frequently connected to dairy but is also contained in small fish that have edible bones, such as sardines.

Fats and Omega Balance: For the health of the heart and brain, Omega-3 fatty acids are highly acknowledged. Although many people identify Omega-3s with flaxseeds or walnuts, the type present in these plants (ALA) is less accessible than the ones present in animal sources, particularly fatty fish. The Omega-6 to Omega-3 ratio in current diets is frequently unbalanced and disproportionately favors Omega-6 fatty acids, even though Omega-6 fatty acids are still important. This equilibrium can be restored by consuming meats that have been grown on pasture and avoiding seed oils.

The Fiber Question: The subject of fiber is arguably one of the most contentious. The digestion benefits of fiber and the ability to reduce cardiovascular risks are highly praised within mainstream nutrition. Even though plants are the main suppliers of fiber, proponents of the carnivore diet contend that fiber is not necessary, citing numerous anecdotal reports of improved gut health and regular bowel movements without it. The foundation of the theory is the idea that when plant-based irritants are absent, the gut can operate at its best without the aid of fiber as a bulking agent. It is a journey of discovery to explore the carnivore diet, where many conventional dietary beliefs are challenged and reexamined. Most vital nutrients are not only met but also optimized with a commitment to understanding and sourcing premium animal products. To ensure that every meal is not only satiating but also deeply nourishing, the key is to approach it with an open mind and knowledge.

Cooking Techniques for Perfect Meat

Meat preparation is a culinary art form that has existed for as long as civilization itself. The taste, texture, and nutritional value of meat can all be significantly impacted by how it is cooked. Whether you're a seasoned cook or a kitchen newbie, learning these techniques will take your meat dishes to a whole new level.

Grilling: Invoking thoughts of open flames and smokey flavors, grilling is possibly the most primitive way to prepare meat. The Maillard process, which takes place at high temperatures when reducing sugars and amino acids are combined, gives meat that special charred flavor when it is grilled over either charcoal or gas. It is ideal for fish, poultry, steak, and hamburgers. To perfect grilling, one must control the heat, guaranteeing even cooking while preserving the meat's juiciness. With high-quality meat, a sprinkle of salt may be all that is necessary. Marinades and rubs can improve flavor.

Roasting: Suitable for larger chunks of meat or whole birds, roasting is a flexible cooking Instructions. Roasting cooks the meat evenly by enclosing it in the dry heat of the oven. The answer in this situation is to cook the inside at a lower temperature while maintaining the tenderness of the outside by starting with a high temperature to sear it. Its juices, herbs, or butter can be used as a basting agent every so often to improve flavor and stop drying out. For foods like prime rib, a whole chicken, or a lamb leg, roasting works best.

Searing: To preserve those flavors, searing is essential. The meat is swiftly cooked in a very hot skillet, resulting in the Maillard reaction's creation of another wonderful brown crust. Due to the way this approach seals in the meat's juices, it frequently precedes other techniques like roasting or slow cooking. To get the perfect crust while searing, you must make sure the pan is hot, the meat surface is dry, and the pan is not overcrowded.

Sous-vide: French for "under vacuum," sous-vide refers to Instructions which seals the meat in bag using vacuum and heated to specific temperatures in a water bath. By doing this, you can guarantee that the meat is cooked thoroughly, that it retains moisture, and that the internal temperature is constant. It's common practice to briefly sear the meat for a delicious crust after sous-vide cooking. The ultimate product—perfectly cooked, delicate meat—is well worth the extra time and effort even if it necessitates special equipment.

Slow Cooking: Slow cooking is all about having patience. Meat is cooked slowly for several hours in a slow cooker or a low-heat oven to allow the flavorful juices to blend and the tough connective fibers to dissolve. For meatier cuts like brisket, shoulder, or ribs that require more effort, use this technique. As a result, the meat is very delicate, easily detachable, and flavorful thanks to the addition of any additional herbs, spices, or liquids.

Every Instructions of cooking has its distinct charm and flavor, transforming a plain piece of meat into a gourmet masterpiece. The approach picked is frequently influenced by the type of meat being used, the desired result, and individual preferences. These Instructions can be mastered with time and effort, ensuring that each meat dish you make is a harmonious blend of flavors, textures, and scents.

Importance of seasoning: The role of salt and other acceptable seasonings

Even the best cuts of meat can benefit from the proper seasoning, which is why the culinary world admires meat for its inherent richness. Consider seasonings as the link that connects the natural flavors of the meat to the tongue, bringing out, balancing, or enhancing the dish's flavors. Many different seasonings can be used, but salt is the most common and is a staple in the kitchen of carnivores.

Salt: The Quintessential Enhancer: A flavor enhancer, salt is more than just a seasoning. Salt improves the flavor of the meat when it is sprinkled on food, in addition to giving it a salty flavor. Since salt helps proteins in meat retain water on a molecular level, it becomes juicier. The Maillard reaction, which produces the savory brown crust on seared or grilled meats, is also aided by this ingredient during cooking. Salt is a vital electrolyte that supports hydration and cellular processes for people who strictly adhere to a carnivorous diet. The addition of trace minerals can also be accomplished by selecting high-quality salts like pink Himalayan salt or sea salt.

Pepper: The Classic Companion: Salt's traditional partner in many meat preparations is pepper, especially black pepper. It adds depth and complexity with its light heat and fragrant scent. The volatile oils released by freshly ground black pepper can enhance even the simplest cuts' flavor profiles.

Garlic and Onions: Flavorful Foundations: Many people find it difficult to ignore the strong aromas of garlic and onions, even if staunch carnivores may choose to forego these. In many different cuisines around the world, they are essential flavoring components. When used sparingly, they can add complexity to a dish's flavor. Sautéed onions add a sweet, caramelized flavor while garlic provides a warm, spicy aroma.

Herbs: Subtle Sophistication: Meats can be flavor-infused with herbs, whether fresh or dried. Lamb dishes can benefit from rosemary's piney flavor, and fowl benefits greatly from thyme's earthy undertones. Fresh herbs may give a burst of flavor and improve the overall profile of a dish when added towards the end of cooking or as a garnish.

Chilies and Spices: Chilies, paprika, and cayenne can be used to add heat if you want something with a little more of a kick, while cumin and coriander can help the flavor profile lean more toward a certain cuisine. To highlight the meat's inherent flavors, these may instead be used sparingly or not at all by the purist. Understanding the character of the meat and combining it with complementary flavors in the right proportions is the art of seasoning. The objective is the same, whether you're a minimalist who likes to let the meat speak for itself or a gourmet explorer who likes to play around with a variety of flavors. Personal preferences are also very important, as they are with all types of art. Finding the ideal spice blend will take some trial and error and palate exploration, but once you do, every mouthful will be a delicious tribute to the marriage of meat and its enhancing Materials.

Safe meat handling, storage, and preparation

Safety is of the utmost importance in a culinary journey that centers on meat. While there are many flavors and nutrients in meat, if it is not handled, kept, or prepared properly, it can also be a potential source of viruses. By navigating this issue, you can have a delicious lunch and feel calm. This detailed guide will show you how to handle meat with care and accuracy.

Shopping and Selection: Start your safety efforts at the source. The least amount of time possible should be spent without refrigeration by placing meat at the end of your shopping list. Make sure the packing is tight and free of rips and leaks. When selecting fresh meat, make sure it is cold to the touch, uniform in color, and smell-free.

Transport and Immediate Storage: Transporting meat from the store to your house should be done in a cooler or an insulated bag, especially in the summer. When you get home, put the meat in the fridge right away and use within days. If not, the freezer is your best option for prolonged storage.

Freezing and Thawing: Meats should only be kept in their original packaging if you plan to freeze them for a brief period to maintain their freshness. Use freezer paper, heavy-duty aluminum foil, or vacuum-sealed bags to rewrap food for extended periods to avoid freezer burn. When defrosting, never do so on the counter; always do it in the refrigerator. By doing this, you may be confident that the meat will defrost at a safe temperature. Use the cold-water approach if you're in a hurry by placing the meat within a waterproof bag and soaking it in water, changing the water every 30 mins. Another option is to defrost the meat in the microwave, but this requires that you cook the meat right away.

Preparation Hygiene: Ensure that your desk is tidy before you begin. Use different cutting boards for meat and other dishes to avoid cross-contamination. Clean and sanitize any surfaces that the meat came into contact with right away, including worktops, knives, and cutting boards. As doing so can transmit infections, avoid rinsing meat in the sink.

Cooking to Safe Temperatures: The most trustworthy Instructions for determining if meat has been cooked to, a safe temperature is to use a food thermometer. The ideal internal temperatures for various types of meat are as follows:

- Poultry (chicken, turkey): 74°C (165°F)
- Ground meats (pork, beef):
- Steaks, roasts, fish: 63°C (145°F)
- Lamb: 63°C (145°F) for medium-rare, 71°C (160°F) for medium.

Further ensuring the eradication of possible viruses is letting meat rest for a short while after cooking.

Storing Leftovers: To avoid condensation, allow cooked meat to cool at room temperature for a short period before putting it in the refrigerator. Shallow containers are best for storing leftovers so they can cool quickly and evenly. For the best quality and safety, eat chilled leftovers within 3–4 days. Depending on the type of meat, it's advisable to eat leftovers as soon as possible after freezing them.

As important to good cooking as seasoning and cooking is treating meat with respect and care. It makes sure that the food you serve is not only tasty but also wholesome. One can enjoy the pleasures of meat with no qualms if one maintains regular routines and pays close attention to every little thing.

Meal Plan

DAY-TO-DAY 2-WEEK MEAL PLAN

Week-1

Day	Breakfast	Lunch	Dinner
Monday	Classic Steak and Eggs	Grilled Bison Burgers	Garlic Butter Roast Chicken
Tuesday	Ostrich Steak with Chimichurri	Salmon and Spinach Curry	Venison Stew
Wednesday	Honey Glazed Salmon	Bison Tacos with Salsa Verde	Teriyaki Ribs
Thursday	Grilled Sardines with Lemon Herb Butter	Sardine and Tomato Pasta	Brisket Tacos
Friday	Ostrich and Vegetable Stir-Fry	Salmon Patties with Dill Sauce	Sunday Roast with Vegetables
Saturday	Bison Chili	Sardine Toast with Avocado	Spiced Ribs with Cumin and Coriander
Sunday	Mackerel with Tomato and Capers	Mackerel and Potato Hash	Spiced Ribs with Cumin and Coriander

Week-2

Day	Breakfast	Lunch	Dinner
Monday	Salmon Ceviche	Bison Meatballs with Tomato Sauce	Mackerel Salad with Mustard Dressing
Tuesday	Venison Sausages with Caramelized Onions	Grilled Ostrich with Garlic Herb Butter	Salmon and Asparagus Foil Packets
Wednesday	Mackerel and Vegetable Stir-Fry	Ostrich Meatballs in Tomato Sauce	Venison and Mushroom Pie
Thursday	Grilled Bison Steaks with Chimichurri	Sardine and Lemon Pasta	Grilled Sardines with Lemon Herb Butter
Friday	Bison Chili	Venison Curry	Mackerel with Tomato and Capers
Saturday	Ostrich Skewers with Pineapple and Peppers	Salmon Patties with Dill Sauce	Honey Glazed Salmon
Sunday	Sardine Salad with Olives	Mackerel and Potato Hash	Bison Meatballs with Tomato Sauce

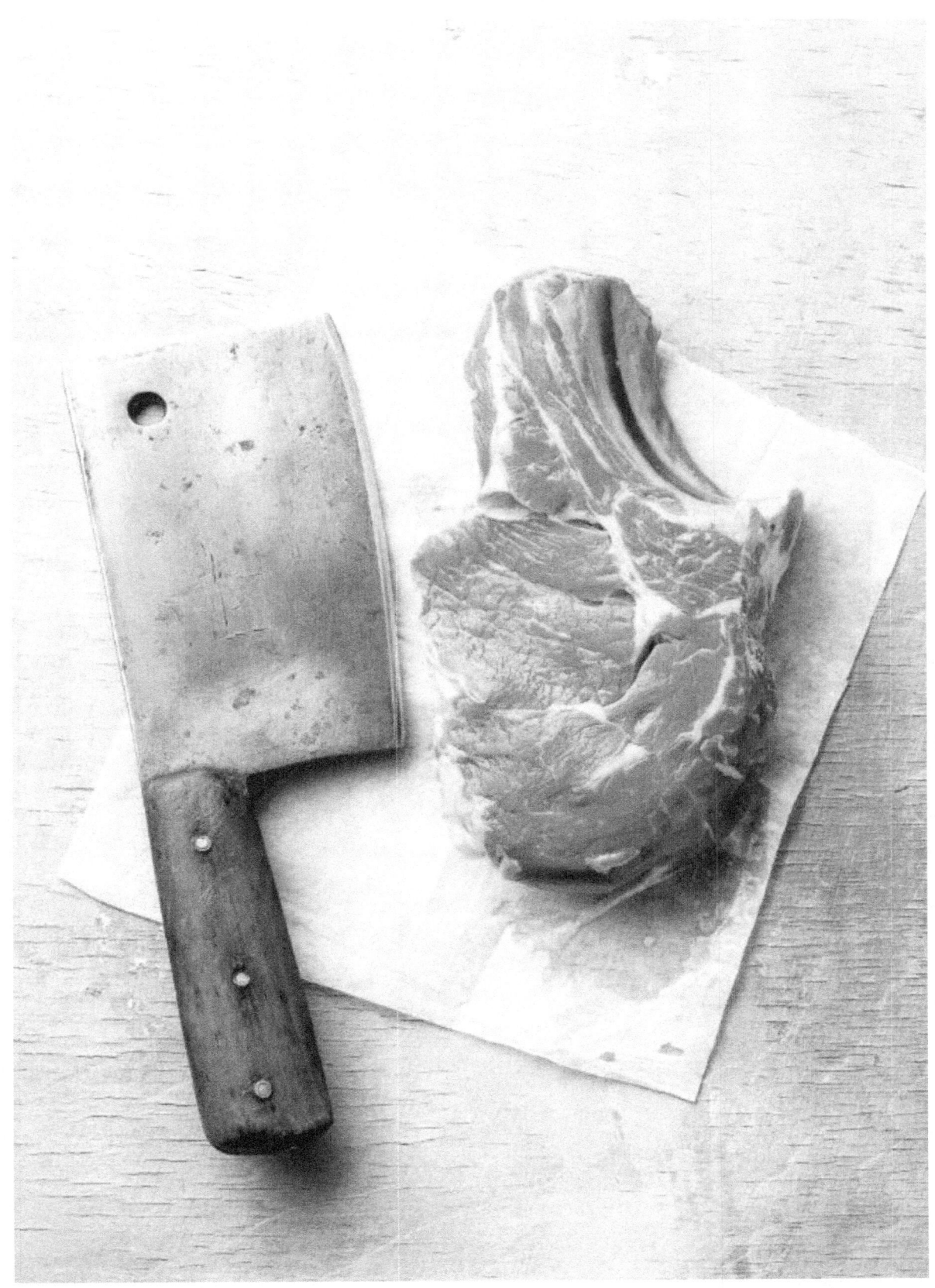

SIMPLE STEAK RECIPES

Basic Grilled Steak

Prep Duration: 10 mins

Cooking: 10 mins

Yield: 2

Materials:

- 2 Steaks of your choice
- 2 tsp of salt
- 2 tsp of black pepper

Method

1. Preheat the grill at high flame.
2. Use pepper and salt to season both sides.
3. Grill each side for about 5 mins.
4. Leave it to rest for 5 mins before slicing.

Nutrient Value: *Energy:* 550, *Fat:* 34g, *Protein:* 52g, *Carbs:* 0g, *Fiber:* 0g

Garlic Butter Steak

Prep Duration: 10 mins

Cooking: 12 mins

Yield: 2

Materials:

- 2 steaks
- 2 tsp of salt
- 2 tsp of black pepper
- 4 garlic cloves, minced
- 4 tbsp unsalted butter

Method

1. Season steaks using pepper and salt.
2. Heat a pan on medium flame. Put in steaks and cook each side for 5-6 mins.
3. Add butter and garlic to the pan and spoon over steaks for 1-2 mins.
4. Leave it for 5 mins well before serving.

Nutrient Value: *Energy:* 650, *Fat:* 42g, *Protein:* 52g, *Carbs:* 3g, *Fiber:* 0g

Pepper Crusted Steak

Prep Duration: 10 mins

Cooking: 10 mins

Yield: 2

Materials:

- 2 steaks
- 2 tbsp coarsely crushed black pepper
- 2 tsp of salt

Method

1. Press crushed pepper onto both sides of the steaks.
2. Season with salt.

3. Grill on both sides for 5 mins.

Nutrient Value: *Energy:* 550, *Fat:* 34g, *Protein:* 52g, *Carbs:* 1g, *Fiber:* 0.5g

Herb Marinated Steak

Prep Duration: 15 mins + 2 hours marinating
Cooking: 10 mins
Yield: 2

Materials:

- 2 steaks
- ¼ cup olive oil
- 2 tsp salt
- 1 tsp black pepper
- 2 garlic cloves, minced
- 1 tbsp rosemary, minced
- 1 tbsp thyme, minced

Method

1. Combine everything (except steaks) in a container.
2. Put steaks in a zip bag and add marinade over. Refrigerate it for 2 hours.
3. Grill steaks 5 mins each side.

Nutrient Value: *Energy:* 660, *Fat:* 46g, *Protein:* 52g, *Carbs:* 1g, *Fiber:* 0g

Asian-inspired Soy Glazed Steak

Prep Duration: 10 mins + 1 hour marinating
Cooking: 10 mins

Yield: 2

Materials:

- 2 steaks
- ¼ cup soy sauce
- 2 tbsp honey
- 2 garlic cloves, minced
- 1 tbsp ginger, minced

Method

1. Mix soy sauce, ginger, honey, and garlic in a container. Marinate steaks for 1 hour.
2. Grill 5 mins each side. Use remaining marinade to baste.

Nutrient Value: *Energy:* 600, *Fat:* 34g, *Protein:* 52g, *Carbs:* 13g, *Fiber:* 0g

Spiced Rubbed Steak

Prep Duration: 10 mins
Cooking: 10 mins
Yield: 2

Materials:

- 2 steaks
- 1 tsp salt
- 1 tsp black pepper
- 1 tsp paprika
- 1 tsp cumin
- 1 tsp garlic powder

Method

1. Mix spices and rub onto steaks.

2. Grill or pan-fry 5 mins each side.

Nutrient Value: *Energy: 560, Fat: 34g, Protein: 52g, Carbs: 2g, Fiber: 1g*

Coffee Crusted Steak

Prep Duration: 10 mins
Cooking: 10 mins
Yield: 2

Materials:

- 2 steaks
- 2 tbsp finely ground coffee
- 1 tsp salt
- 1 tsp brown sugar
- ½ tsp black pepper

Method

1. Mix coffee, salt, sugar, and pepper. Press onto steaks.
2. Grill or pan-fry 5 mins each side.

Nutrient Value: *Energy: 570, Fat: 34g, Protein: 52g, Carbs: 4g, Fiber: 0g*

Lemon Herb Steak

Prep Duration: 10 mins + 1 hour marinating
Cooking: 10 mins
Yield: 2

Materials:

- 2 steaks
- Juice of 1 lemon
- Zest of 1 lemon
- 1 tsp salt

- 2 tbsp olive oil
- 1 tbsp chopped parsley
- 1 garlic clove, minced

Method

1. Combine all ingredients (except steaks) in a container. Let it rest for for 1 hour.
2. Grill 5 mins each side.

Nutrient Value: *Energy: 620, Fat: 40g, Protein: 52g, Carbs: 2g, Fiber: 0g*

Balsamic Glazed Steak

Prep Duration: 10 mins + 1 hour marinating
Cooking: 12 mins
Yield: 2

Materials:

- 2 steaks
- ¼ cup balsamic vinegar
- 2 tbsp honey
- 1 garlic clove, minced
- Salt and pepper to taste

Method

1. Mix vinegar, pepper, garlic, salt, and honey. Marinate steaks for one hour.
2. Grill the steaks for 5 mins on both side, basting with remaining marinade.

Nutrient Value: *Energy: 600, Fat: 34g, Protein: 52g, Carbs: 15g, Fiber: 0*

Chimichurri Steak

Prep Duration: 15 mins

Cooking: 10 mins

Yield: 2

Materials:

- 2 steaks
- ½ cup fresh parsley, chopped
- 4 garlic cloves, minced
- ¼ cup olive oil
- 2 tbsp red wine vinegar
- 1 tsp red pepper flakes
- Salt to taste

Method

1. Mix parsley, olive oil, red pepper flakes,salt, garlic, and vinegar for the chimichurri sauce.
2. Grill the steaks for 5 mins on both the side.
3. Serve with chimichurri sauce drizzled over.

Nutrient Value: *Energy:* 670, *Fat:* 45g, *Protein:* 52g, *Carbs:* 3g, *Fiber:*

GROUND MEAT DISHES

Classic Meatballs

Prep Duration: 15 mins
Cooking: 20 mins
Yield: 4

Materials:

- 1 lb. ground beef
- 1/4 cup breadcrumbs
- 1 egg
- 2 tbsp parsley, chopped
- 1 garlic clove, minced
- Salt and pepper to taste
- 1 cup marinara sauce

Method

1. Mix beef, breadcrumbs, egg, pepper, garlic, salt, and parsley. Shape into one inch balls.
2. Heat marinara inside a skillet and add meatballs.
3. Cook it thoroughly for 20 minutes or until browned.

Nutrient Value: *Energy:* 290, *Fat:* 17g, *Protein:* 25g, *Carbs:* 8g, *Fiber:* 1g

Beef Tacos

Prep Duration: 10 mins
Cooking: 15 mins
Yield: 4

Materials:

- 1 lb. ground beef
- 1 packet taco seasoning
- 8 taco shells
- Toppings: lettuce, cheese, tomatoes, etc.

Method

1. Cook beef in a pan till it is browned. Remove fat.
2. Put in taco seasoning and cook as directed.
3. Serve in taco shells with toppings.

Nutrient Value: *Energy:* 410, *Fat:* 23g, *Protein:* 22g, *Carbs:* 28g, *Fiber:* 3g

Meatloaf

Prep Duration: 15 mins
Cooking: 55 mins
Yield: 6

Materials:

- 1 lb. ground beef
- 1/2 cup breadcrumbs
- 1/4 cup milk
- 1 egg
- 1/4 cup ketchup
- 1 onion, chopped
- Salt and pepper to taste

Method

1. Preheat the oven to (375°F).
2. Combine all the material and shape into a loaf.
3. Bake for 55 mins or till done.

Nutrient Value: *Energy:* 320, *Fat:* 18g, *Protein:* 22g, *Carbs:* 16g, *Fiber:* 1g

Salisbury Steak

Prep Duration: 20 mins

Cooking: 25 mins

Yield: 4

Materials:

- 1 lb. ground beef
- 1/4 cup breadcrumbs
- 1 egg
- Salt and pepper
- 1 cup beef broth
- 1 onion, sliced
- 1 tbsp cornstarch

Method

1. Mix beef, breadcrumbs, egg, salt, and pepper. Make them into 4 patties.
2. Cook patties in skillet until browned. Remove.
3. Add onions and sauté. Add broth and return patties.
4. Cook until patties are done, about 15 mins.
5. Combine cornstarch with little water and put in to thicken sauce.

Nutrient Value: *Energy:* 300, *Fat:* 16g, *Protein:* 25g, *Carbs:* 12g, *Fiber:* 1g

Chili

Prep Duration: 15 mins

Cooking: 45 mins

Yield: 6

Materials:

- 1 lb. ground beef
- 1 can (15 oz.) kidney beans, drained
- 1 can (15 oz.) diced tomatoes
- 1 onion, chopped
- 2 tbsp chili powder
- Salt and pepper

Method

1. Brown beef with onions in a pot.
2. Add salt, tomatoes, chili powder, beans, and pepper.
3. Simmer for 45 mins.

Nutrient Value: *Energy:* 350, *Fat:* 14g, *Protein:* 24g, *Carbs:* 28g, *Fiber:* 7g

Stuffed Peppers

Prep Duration: 20 mins

Cooking: 40 mins

Yield: 4

Materials:

- 4 bell peppers, tops removed and seeds scooped out
- 1 lb. ground beef
- 1/2 cup cooked rice
- 1 can (15 oz.) diced tomatoes
- 1 garlic clove, minced
- Salt and pepper

Method

1. Preheat oven to 375°F (190°C).
2. Mix beef, rice, half of the tomatoes, garlic, salt, and pepper.
3. Add meat mix in pepper and put them in baking tray.
4. Pour remaining tomatoes over peppers.
5. Bake for 40 mins.

Nutrient Value: *Energy:* 310, *Fat:* 14g, *Protein:* 23g, *Carbs:* 22g, *Fiber:* 3g

Swedish Meatballs

Prep Duration: 20 mins
Cooking: 20 mins
Yield: 4

Materials:

- 1 lb. ground beef
- 1/4 cup breadcrumbs
- 1/4 cup milk
- 1 egg
- 1 onion, finely chopped
- 2 cups beef broth
- 1/4 cup heavy cream
- Salt and pepper
- 1 tbsp butter

Method

1. Mix beef, breadcrumbs, salt, egg, pepper, milk, and onion. Shape into small balls.
2. Brown meatballs in butter in a pan.
3. Add broth and let it heat for 10 mins.
4. Put in cream and cook for another 10 mins.

Nutrient Value: *Energy:* 390, *Fat:* 24g, *Protein:* 26g, *Carbs:* 15g, *Fiber:* 1g

Spaghetti Bolognese

Prep Duration: 20 mins
Cooking: 45 mins
Yield: 4

Materials:

- 1 lb. ground beef
- 1 can (28 oz.) crushed tomatoes
- 1 onion, chopped
- 2 garlic cloves, minced
- 2 tsp basil
- 2 tsp oregano
- Salt and pepper
- Cooked spaghetti

Method

1. Brown beef, onion, and garlic in a pot.
2. Add tomatoes, basil, oregano, salt, and pepper.
3. Simmer for 45 mins. Serve over spaghetti.

Nutrient Value: *Energy:* 420, *Fat:* 14g, *Protein:* 25g, *Carbs:* 45g, *Fiber:* 4g

Sloppy Joes

Prep Duration: 10 mins
Cooking: 20 mins
Yield: 4

Materials:

- 1 lb. ground beef
- 1/2 cup ketchup
- 2 tbsp brown sugar
- 1 tbsp mustard
- 1 onion, chopped
- 4 hamburger buns

Method

1. Brown beef and onion in a skillet.
2. Add ketchup, brown sugar, and mustard. Simmer for 20 mins.
3. Serve on buns.

Nutrient Value: *Energy:* 390, *Fat:* 15g, *Protein:* 23g, *Carbs:* 40g, *Fiber:* 1g

Beef Burritos

Prep Duration: 15 mins
Cooking: 20 mins
Yield: 4

Materials:

- 1 lb. ground beef
- 1 packet taco seasoning
- 1 can (15 oz.) refried beans
- 4 large tortillas
- Toppings: cheese, lettuce, sour cream, etc.

Method

1. Cook beef in a pan. Put in taco seasoning and cook as directed.
2. Warm beans and place them on tortillas.
3. Add beef and toppings. Roll up.

Nutrient Value: *Energy:* 490, *Fat:* 22g, *Protein:* 28g, *Carbs:* 42g, *Fiber:* 6g

Beef and Broccoli Stir-Fry

Prep Duration: 20 mins
Cooking: 15 mins
Yield: 4

Materials:

- 1 lb. ground beef
- 2 cups broccoli florets
- 1/4 cup soy sauce
- 2 tbsp brown sugar

- 1 garlic clove, minced
- 1 tbsp oil

Method

1. In a pan, warm the oil and brown beef.
2. Add broccoli and fry for 5 mins.
3. Mix soy sauce, garlic, and brown sugar. Add to skillet and cook for about more 5 mins.

Nutrient Value: *Energy:* 360, *Fat:* 18g, *Protein:* 28g, *Carbs:* 20g, *Fiber:* 2g

Meaty Quesadillas

Prep Duration: 15 mins
Cooking: 15 mins
Yield: 4

Materials:

- 1 lb. ground beef
- 1 packet taco seasoning
- 4 large tortillas
- 1 cup cheddar cheese, shredded
- 1/2 cup salsa

Method

1. Cook beef in a skillet. Put in taco seasoning and cook as directed.
2. Spread beef and cheese on half of each tortilla. Fold over.
3. Cook in a skillet until browned and crispy. Serve with salsa.

Nutrient Value: *Energy:* 450, *Fat:* 24g, *Protein:* 30g, *Carbs:* 30g, *Fiber:* 2g

Beef and Mushroom Pie

Prep Duration: 25 mins
Cooking: 30 mins
Yield: 6

Materials:

- 1 lb. ground beef
- 1 cup mushrooms, sliced
- 1 onion, chopped
- 1 cup beef broth
- 1 pie crust
- Salt and pepper

Method

1. Brown beef, mushrooms, and onion in a pan.
2. Put in broth, salt, and pepper. Simmer for 15 mins.
3. Put it into a pie dish and place on pie crust
4. Bake for half an hour at 375°F (190°C) until crust is golden.

Nutrient Value: *Energy:* 360, *Fat:* 20g, *Protein:* 20g, *Carbs:* 22g, *Fiber:* 1g

Cottage Pie

Prep Duration: 30 mins
Cooking: 30 mins
Yield: 6

Materials:

- 1 lb. ground beef
- 1 onion, chopped
- 2 carrots, chopped
- 1 cup beef broth
- 2 cups mashed potatoes
- Salt and pepper

Method

1. Brown beef, onion, and carrots in a pan.
2. Put in broth, salt, and pepper. Simmer for 15 mins.
3. Put it in a baking dish andplace mashed potatoes on top.
4. Bake for half an hour at 375°F or till top is golden.

Nutrient Value: *Energy:* 340, *Fat:* 14g, *Protein:* 18g, *Carbs:* 34g, *Fiber:* 3g

Beef Kofta Kebabs

Prep Duration: 25 mins

Cooking: 15 mins

Yield: 4

Materials:

- 1 lb. ground beef
- 1/4 cup breadcrumbs
- 1 onion, finely chopped
- 2 garlic cloves, minced
- 1 tsp cumin
- 1 tsp coriander
- Salt and pepper

Method

1. Combine all materials and make elongated kebabs around skewers.
2. Grill or broil until cooked through.

Nutrient Value: *Energy:* 290, *Fat:* 14g, *Protein:* 25g, *Carbs:* 14g, *Fiber:* 1g

ORGAN MEAT: LIVER, HEART, KIDNEY RECIPES

Classic Liver and Onions

Prep Duration: 10 mins

Cooking: 20 mins

Yield: 4

Materials:

- 1 lb. beef liver, sliced
- 2 onions, thinly sliced
- 2 tbsp butter
- Salt and pepper

Method

1. Melt butter in a pan.
2. Put in onions and let it cook until softened.
3. Add liver slices and cook until browned on each side.
4. Add the seasonings.

Nutrient Value: *Energy:* 220, *Fat:* 10g, *Protein:* 26g, *Carbs:* 6g, *Fiber:* 1g

Chicken Liver Pâté

Prep Duration: 15 mins

Cooking: 25 mins

Yield: 6

Materials:

- 1 lb. chicken livers
- 1 onion, chopped
- 2 garlic cloves, minced
- 1/2 cup butter
- 1/4 cup brandy
- Salt and pepper

Method

1. Put garlic and onion in buttered pan and saute until translucent.
2. Add livers and cook until browned.
3. Put in brandy and cook for 5 more mins.
4. Blend till smooth in a food processor.
5. Add the seasonings.

Nutrient Value: *Energy:* 290, *Fat:* 23g, *Protein:* 16g, *Carbs:* 3g, *Fiber:* 0g

Grilled Beef Heart

Prep Duration: 10 mins + 2 hours marinating

Cooking: 15 mins

Yield: 4

Materials:

- 1 beef heart, sliced

- 1/4 cup olive oil
- 2 garlic cloves, minced
- 1 tsp oregano
- Salt and pepper

Method

1. Marinate heart slices in olive oil, garlic, oregano, salt, and pepper for 2 hours.
2. Grill until browned on both sides.

Nutrient Value: *Energy:* 250, *Fat:* 12g, *Protein:* 30g, *Carbs:* 2g, *Fiber:* 0g

Kidney Stew

Prep Duration: 20 mins
Cooking: 1 hour 15 mins
Yield: 6

Materials:

- 1 lb. beef kidneys, diced
- 1 onion, chopped
- 2 carrots, sliced
- 2 potatoes, diced
- 4 cups beef broth
- Salt and pepper

Method

1. Cook onion in a pot till translucent.
2. Put in the kidneys and brown.
3. Add broth, carrots, as well as potatoes.
4. Let it simmer for 1 hour.
5. Add the seasonings.

Nutrient Value: *Energy:* 210, *Fat:* 5g, *Protein:* 20g, *Carbs:* 20g, *Fiber:* 3g

Heart and Mushroom Pie

Prep Duration: 25 mins
Cooking: 45 mins
Yield: 6

Materials:

- 1 lb. beef heart, diced
- 1 cup mushrooms, sliced
- 1 onion, chopped
- 1 cup beef broth
- 1 pie crust
- Salt and pepper

Method

1. Brown heart, mushrooms, and onion in a pan.
2. Put in the broth, salt, and pepper.
3. Add it in a pie dish and top with pie crust.
4. Bake at 375°F (190°C) until crust is golden.

Nutrient Value: *Energy:* 340, *Fat:* 18g, *Protein:* 22g, *Carbs:* 22g, *Fiber:* 2g

Liver Dumplings Soup

Prep Duration: 30 mins
Cooking: 25 mins
Yield: 6

Materials:

- 1/2 lb. beef liver, minced
- 1/2 cup breadcrumbs
- 1 egg
- 6 cups beef broth
- 2 tbsp parsley, chopped
- Salt and pepper

Method

1. Combine liver, breadcrumbs, egg, parsley, salt, and pepper to form dumplings.
2. Bring broth to a boil, add dumplings, and simmer for 25 mins.

Nutrient Value: *Energy:* 150, *Fat:* 5g, *Protein:* 12g, *Carbs:* 10g, *Fiber:* 1g

Kidney Beans and Kidneys

Prep Duration: 15 mins
Cooking: 35 mins
Yield: 4

Materials:

- 1 lb. beef kidneys, diced
- 1 can (15 oz.) kidney beans, drained
- 1 onion, chopped
- 2 garlic cloves, minced
- 1 cup beef broth
- Salt and pepper

Method

1. Brown kidneys, onion, and garlic in a skillet.
2. Put in broth, beans, salt, and pepper.
3. Simmer for 30 mins.

Nutrient Value: *Energy:* 280, *Fat:* 8g, *Protein:* 28g, *Carbs:* 24g, *Fiber:* 7g

Grilled Heart Skewers

Prep Duration: 15 mins + 2 hours marinating
Cooking: 15 mins
Yield: 4

Materials:

- 1 beef heart, cubed
- 1/4 cup soy sauce
- 1 tbsp honey
- 2 garlic cloves, minced
- 1 tsp ginger, minced

Method

1. Marinate heart cubes in soy sauce, honey, garlic, and ginger for 2 hours.
2. Thread onto skewers and grill until browned.

Nutrient Value: *Energy:* 200, *Fat:* 6g, *Protein:* 28g, *Carbs:* 10g, *Fiber:* 0g

Liver in Cream Sauce

Prep Duration: 10 mins

Cooking: 25 mins

Yield: 4

Materials:

- 1 lb. beef liver, sliced
- 1 onion, thinly sliced
- 1 cup heavy cream
- 2 tbsp butter
- Salt and pepper

Method

1. Put butter in a skillet.
2. Put in onions and cook it till soft.
3. Put in liver slices and let it cook until browned.
4. Add cream and have it simmer for 10 mins.
5. Ass the seasonings.

Nutrient Value: *Energy:* 380, *Fat:* 28g, *Protein:* 26g, *Carbs:* 6g, *Fiber:* 1g

Kidney Curry

Prep Duration: 20 mins

Cooking: 35 mins

Yield: 4

Materials:

- 1 lb. beef kidneys, diced
- 1 onion, chopped
- 2 tbsp curry powder
- 1 can (15 oz.) diced tomatoes
- 1/2 cup yogurt
- Salt and pepper

Method

1. Brown kidneys and onion in a skillet.
2. Add curry powder and tomatoes.
3. Simmer for 30 mins.
4. Add in the yogurt and seasonings.

Nutrient Value: *Energy:* 220, *Fat:* 8g, *Protein:* 24g, *Carbs:* 12g, *Fiber:* 3g

Heart Tacos

Prep Duration: 15 mins

Cooking: 20 mins

Yield: 4

Materials:

- 1 beef heart, diced
- 1 packet taco seasoning
- 8 taco shells
- Toppings: lettuce, cheese, tomatoes, etc.

Method

1. Cook diced heart in skillet until browned.
2. Add taco seasoning and cook as directed.
3. Serve in taco shells with toppings.

Nutrient Value: *Energy:* 250, *Fat:* 10g, *Protein:* 20g, *Carbs:* 20g, *Fiber:* 3g

Liver Stuffed Bell Peppers

Prep Duration: 20 mins

Cooking: 40 mins

Yield: 4

Materials:

- 4 bell peppers, tops removed and seeds scooped out
- 1/2 lb. beef liver, minced
- 1/2 lb. ground beef
- 1 onion, chopped
- 1 garlic clove, minced
- 1 cup beef broth
- Salt and pepper

Method

1. Brown liver, beef, onion, as well as garlic in a pan.
2. Add broth and simmer for 10 mins.
3. Stuff mixture into peppers and bake for 30 mins at 375°F.

Nutrient Value: *Energy:* 280, *Fat:* 14g, *Protein:* 24g, *Carbs:* 14g, *Fiber:* 3g

Kidney and Mushroom Risotto

Prep Duration: 20 mins

Cooking: 40 mins

Yield: 4

Materials:

- 1/2 lb. beef kidneys, diced
- 1 cup arborio rice
- 1 onion, chopped
- 1 cup mushrooms, sliced
- 4 cups beef broth, warmed
- 2 tbsp butter
- Salt and pepper

Method

1. Melt butter within a pot and sauté kidneys, mushrooms, and onion.
2. Add rice and stir.
3. Gradually add broth, stirring until rice is creamy and cooked.
4. Put in the seasonings.

Nutrient Value: *Energy:* 380, *Fat:* 10g, *Protein:* 20g, *Carbs:* 50g, *Fiber:* 2g

Heart and Potato Hash

Prep Duration: 15 mins

Cooking: 25 mins

Yield: 4

Materials:

- 1 beef heart, diced
- 2 potatoes, diced
- 1 onion, chopped
- 2 tbsp oil
- Salt and pepper

Method

1. Take a pan and warm oil in it.
2. Put in heart, potatoes, and onion.
3. Cook until potatoes are browned and heart is cooked.

4. Season with salt and pepper.

Nutrient Value: *Energy:* 290, *Fat:* 10g, *Protein:* 20g, *Carbs:* 30g, *Fiber:* 3g

Chicken Liver Fried Rice

Prep Duration: 20 mins

Cooking: 20 mins

Yield: 4

Materials:

- 1/2 lb. chicken livers, diced
- 2 cups cooked rice
- 1 onion, chopped
- 2 eggs, beaten
- 2 tbsp soy sauce
- 1 tbsp oil

Method

1. Heat oil in a pan.
2. Put in onion and liver, let it cook till liver is browned.
3. Push to a side and scramble eggs in other side.
4. Put in rice and soy sauce, stir everything together.

Nutrient Value: *Energy:* 310, *Fat:* 8g, *Protein:* 18g, *Carbs:* 40g, *Fiber:* 1g

BONE BROTH

Classic Bone Broth

Prep Duration: 15 mins

Cooking: 24 hours

Yield: 8

Materials:

- 2 lb. mixed beef bones
- 1 onion, quartered
- 2 carrots, chopped
- 2 celery stalks, chopped
- 2 garlic cloves
- 1 bay leaf
- 2 tbsp apple cider vinegar
- Salt and pepper
- 10 cups water

Method

1. Mix all materials in a big pot.
2. Let it boil and then simmer for 24 hours.
3. Strain and store in refrigerator.

Nutrient Value: *Energy:* 30, *Fat:* 1g, *Protein:* 2g, *Carbs:* 3g, *Fiber:* 0g

Chicken Bone Broth

Prep Duration: 15 mins

Cooking: 12 hours

Yield: 8

Materials:

- 1 whole chicken carcass
- 1 onion, quartered
- 2 carrots, chopped
- 2 celery stalks, chopped
- 2 garlic cloves
- 1 bay leaf
- 2 tbsp apple cider vinegar
- Salt and pepper
- 10 cups water

Method

1. Put all the materials in a big skillet.
2. .
3. Let it boil and then simmer for 12 hours.
4. Strain and refrigerate.

Nutrient Value: *Energy:* 25, *Fat:* 0.5g, *Protein:* 1g, *Carbs:* 3g, *Fiber:* 0g

Bone Broth Ramen

Prep Duration: 10 mins

Cooking: 15 mins

Yield: 4

Materials:

- 4 cups beef bone broth
- 4 packets of ramen noodles
- 2 green onions, sliced

- 1 carrot, julienned
- 1/2 cup sliced mushrooms
- 1 tbsp soy sauce
- 1 tsp sesame oil

Method

1. Heat bone broth in a pan.
2. Put in ramen and let it cook until soft.
3. Stir in soy sauce, sesame oil, green onions, carrot, and mushrooms.
4. Serve hot.

Nutrient Value: *Energy: 210, Fat: 7g, Protein: 8g, Carbs: 28g, Fiber: 2g*

Spiced Bone Broth

Prep Duration: 10 mins

Cooking: 24 hours

Yield: 8

Materials:

- 2 lb. mixed beef bones
- 10 cups water
- 2 tbsp apple cider vinegar
- 1 tsp turmeric
- 1 tsp ginger
- 1/2 tsp black pepper
- Salt

Method

1. Mix all Materials in a big pot.
2. .
3. Let it boil and then simmer for 24 hours.

4. Strain and store.

Nutrient Value: *Energy: 30, Fat: 1g, Protein: 2g, Carbs: 2g, Fiber: 0g*

Bone Broth Soup with Vegetables

Prep Duration: 15 mins

Cooking: 30 mins

Yield: 6

Materials:

- 6 cups chicken bone broth
- 2 carrots, sliced
- 1 onion, diced
- 2 celery stalks, sliced
- 1 cup diced tomatoes
- 1/2 cup chopped kale
- Salt and pepper

Method

1. Boil bone broth in a pot.
2. Put in vegetables and simmer until soft.
3. Add the seasonings.

Nutrient Value: *Energy: 50, Fat: 0.5g, Protein: 4g, Carbs: 8g, Fiber: 1g*

Creamy Bone Broth Pasta

Prep Duration: 10 mins

Cooking: 20 mins

Yield: 4

Materials:

- 4 cups beef bone broth
- 8 oz. pasta
- 1/2 cup heavy cream
- 1/4 cup grated Parmesan cheese
- 2 garlic cloves, minced
- Salt and pepper

Method

1. Boil pasta in bone broth until al dente.
2. Reduce flame, add heavy cream, Parmesan, and garlic.
3. Simmer until sauce thickens.
4. Season it well.

Nutrient Value: *Energy:* 310, *Fat:* 14g, *Protein:* 12g, *Carbs:* 35g, *Fiber:* 1g

Bone Broth and Lentil Soup

Prep Duration: 15 mins

Cooking: 45 mins

Yield: 6

Materials:

- 6 cups beef bone broth
- 1 cup green lentils
- 1 onion, diced
- 2 carrots, sliced
- 1 celery stalk, chopped
- 2 garlic cloves, minced
- Salt and pepper

Method

1. Bring broth to a boil, put in lentils, vegetables, and garlic.
2. Simmer for 45 mins, or till lentils are soft.
3. Add the seasonings.

Nutrient Value: *Energy:* 120, *Fat:* 0.5g, *Protein:* 9g, *Carbs:* 20g, *Fiber:* 8g

Bone Broth and Quinoa Porridge

Prep Duration: 5 mins

Cooking: 25 mins

Yield: 4

Materials:

- 4 cups chicken bone broth
- 1 cup quinoa
- 1/2 tsp salt
- Green onions for garnish

Method

1. Boil the broth.
2. Put in quinoa as well as salt.
3. Let it simmer for 20 mins at low heat, or till quinoa is cooked.
4. Garnish with green onions.

Nutrient Value: *Energy:* 150, *Fat:* 2g, *Protein:* 8g, *Carbs:* 25g, *Fiber:* 3g

Spicy Bone Broth with Ginger and Chili

Prep Duration: 10 mins

Cooking: 24 hours

Yield: 8

Materials:

- 2 lb. mixed beef bones
- 10 cups water
- 2 tbsp apple cider vinegar
- 1 piece of ginger, sliced
- 1 chili, sliced
- Salt

Method

1. Combine all Materials in a container.
2. Boil it and then simmer for 24 hours at low flame.
3. Strain and season with salt.

Nutrient Value: *Energy:* 30, *Fat:* 1g, *Protein:* 2g, *Carbs:* 2g, *Fiber:* 0g

Bone Broth and Vegetable Stir-Fry

Prep Duration: 20 mins

Cooking: 15 mins

Yield: 4

Materials:

- 1 cup beef bone broth
- 2 tbsp soy sauce
- 2 tbsp oyster sauce
- 1 tbsp cornstarch
- 1 cup broccoli florets
- 1 red bell pepper, sliced
- 1 carrot, sliced
- 1 tbsp oil

Method

1. Warm oil in a pan.
2. Put in the vegetables and cook till soft.
3. Mix oyster sauce, soy sauce, bone broth, and cornstarch in a container.
4. Pour over vegetables and cook until sauce thickens.

Nutrient Value: *Energy:* 80, *Fat:* 3.5g, *Protein:* 3g, *Carbs:* 10g, *Fiber:* 2g

Bone Broth Smoothie

Prep Duration: 5 mins

Cooking: 0 mins

Yield: 1

Materials:

- 1 cup chicken bone broth, chilled
- 1/2 banana
- 1/2 cup spinach
- 1 tbsp chia seeds

Method

1. Mix all Materials using a blender till smooth.

Nutrient Value: *Energy:* 130, *Fat:* 3g, *Protein:* 6g, *Carbs:* 20g, *Fiber:* 4g

Bone Broth Miso Soup

Prep Duration: 10 mins
Cooking: 15 mins
Yield: 4

Materials:

- 4 cups chicken bone broth
- 3 tbsp miso paste
- 1/2 cup tofu, cubed
- 2 green onions, sliced

Method

1. Heat broth in a pot but do not boil.
2. Take a cup of broth and dissolve miso paste in it.
3. Return to the pot.
4. Add tofu and green onions.
5. Serve warm.

Nutrient Value: *Energy:* 90, *Fat:* 2.5g, *Protein:* 7g, *Carbs:* 8g, *Fiber:* 1g

Bone Broth Risotto

Prep Duration: 10 mins
Cooking: 30 mins
Yield: 4

Materials:

- 1 cup arborio rice
- 4 cups beef bone broth
- 1/2 cup Parmesan cheese, grated
- 1 onion, diced
- 2 garlic cloves, minced
- 2 tbsp butter
- Salt and pepper

Method

1. Stir fry garlic and onion in butter.
2. Put in rice and toast for few mins.
3. Gradually put in the broth, stirring constantly, until rice is creamy.
4. Add the cheese and seasonings.

Nutrient Value: *Energy:* 310, *Fat:* 10g, *Protein:* 10g, *Carbs:* 45g, *Fiber:* 1g

Bone Broth and Cabbage Soup

Prep Duration: 10 mins
Cooking: 25 mins
Yield: 6

Materials:

- 6 cups beef bone broth
- 1/2 head cabbage, chopped
- 2 carrots, sliced
- 1 onion, diced
- Salt and pepper

Method

1. Boil the broth, add vegetables, and simmer until tender.
2. Season with salt and pepper.

Nutrient Value: *Energy:* 50, *Fat:* 1g, *Protein:* 4g, *Carbs:* 8g, *Fiber:* 2g

Bone Broth and Tomato Soup

Prep Duration: 10 mins

Cooking: 30 mins

Yield: 4

Materials:

- 2 cups beef bone broth
- 2 cups crushed tomatoes
- 1 onion, diced
- 2 garlic cloves, minced
- 1 tsp basil
- Salt and pepper
- 1 tbsp oil

Method

1. Warm the oil in a pan to stir fry onion and garlic.
2. Put in tomatoes, broth, as well as basil.
3. Cook for 30 mins.
4. Add seasonings

Nutrient Value: *Energy:* 70, *Fat:* 3g, *Protein:* 3g, *Carbs:* 9g, *Fiber:* 2g

RIBS, BRISKETS, AND ROASTS

Classic BBQ Pork Ribs

Prep Duration: 15 mins

Cooking: 3 hours

Yield: 4

Materials:

- 2 lb. pork ribs
- 2 cups BBQ sauce
- Salt and pepper

Method

1. Put in salt and pepper on ribs.
2. Bake in a 275°F (135°C) oven for 2.5 hours.
3. Glaze with BBQ sauce and grill for 15 mins.

Nutrient Value: *Energy:* 620, *Fat:* 34g, *Protein:* 50g, *Carbs:* 30g, *Fiber:* 0g

Beef Brisket with Gravy

Prep Duration: 20 mins

Cooking: 4 hours

Yield: 6

Materials:

- 3 lb. beef brisket
- 1 onion, sliced
- 3 cups beef broth
- 2 tbsp flour
- Salt and pepper

Method

1. Season brisket.
2. Put it in a roasting pan along onions.
3. Add broth and cover.
4. Cook in a 325°F (165°C) oven for 3.5 hours.
5. For gravy, mix pan juices with flour.

Nutrient Value: *Energy:* 480, *Fat:* 30g, *Protein:* 40g, *Carbs:* 5g, *Fiber:* 1g

Garlic Herb Roast Beef

Prep Duration: 20 mins

Cooking: 1 hour

Yield: 6

Materials:

- 3 lb. beef roast
- 4 garlic cloves, minced
- 2 tsp rosemary
- 2 tsp thyme
- Salt and pepper

Method

1. Rub beef with pepper, rosemary, garlic, salt, and thyme.
2. Put it in a 375°F (190°C) oven for 1 hour or until desired doneness.

Nutrient Value: *Energy:* 420, *Fat:* 28g, *Protein:* 36g, *Carbs:* 1g, *Fiber:* 0g

Spicy Honey Glazed Ribs

Prep Duration: 15 mins

Cooking: 3 hours

Yield: 4

Materials:

- 2 lb. pork ribs
- 1/2 cup honey
- 1/4 cup chili sauce
- Salt and pepper

Method

1. Season ribs with salt and pepper.
2. Mix honey and chili sauce.
3. Bake ribs in a 275°F (135°C) oven for 2.5 hours.
4. Glaze with honey mixture and grill for 15 mins.

Nutrient Value: *Energy:* 630, *Fat:* 34g, *Protein:* 48g, *Carbs:* 35g, *Fiber:* 0g

Slow-Cooked Brisket Sandwiches

Prep Duration: 20 mins

Cooking: 8 hours

Yield: 6

Materials:

- 3 lb. beef brisket
- 2 cups BBQ sauce
- 6 buns
- Salt and pepper

Method

1. Season brisket and place in a slow cooker.
2. Put in the BBQ sauce.
3. Cook for 8 hours on low flame.
4. Shred and serve on buns.

Nutrient Value: *Energy:* 530, *Fat:* 22g, *Protein:* 40g, *Carbs:* 40g, *Fiber:* 1g

Pot Roast with Veggies

Prep Duration: 25 mins

Cooking: 4 hours

Yield: 6

Materials:

- 3 lb. beef roast
- 3 carrots, chopped
- 3 potatoes, diced
- 1 onion, chopped
- 4 cups beef broth
- Salt and pepper

Method

1. Season beef and place in a big container.
2. Put in veggies and broth.
3. Put on the lid and simmer for 4 hours.

Nutrient Value: *Energy:* 460, *Fat:* 20g, *Protein:* 40g, *Carbs:* 30g, *Fiber:* 5g

Sticky Asian Ribs

Prep Duration: 20 mins

Cooking: 2.5 hours

Yield: 4

Materials:

- 2 lb. pork ribs
- 1/4 cup soy sauce
- 1/4 cup honey
- 2 tbsp rice vinegar
- 1 tbsp ginger, minced

Method

1. Mix soy sauce, honey, vinegar, and ginger.
2. Glaze ribs with the mixture.
3. Bake in a 275°F (135°C) oven for 2.5 hours.

Nutrient Value: *Energy:* 620, *Fat:* 34g, *Protein:* 50g, *Carbs:* 32g, *Fiber:* 0g

Brisket Chili

Prep Duration: 25 mins

Cooking: 3 hours

Yield: 6

Materials:

- 2 lb. beef brisket, diced
- 1 onion, chopped
- 2 garlic cloves, minced
- 2 cans (15 oz.) kidney beans
- 1 can (15 oz.) diced tomatoes
- 2 tbsp chili powder
- Salt and pepper

Method

1. Brown brisket, onion, and garlic.
2. Add beans, tomatoes, and chili powder.
3. Simmer for 3 hours.
4. Add the seasonings.

Nutrient Value: *Energy:* 390, *Fat:* 18g, *Protein:* 30g, *Carbs:* 30g, *Fiber:* 7g

Herb Crusted Roast Lamb

Prep Duration: 20 mins

Cooking: 1.5 hours

Yield: 6

Materials:

- 3 lb. lamb roast
- 4 garlic cloves, minced
- 2 tsp rosemary
- 2 tsp thyme
- Salt and pepper

Method

1. Rub lamb with pepper, rosemary, thyme, salt, and garlic.
2. Put in a 375°F (190°C) oven for 1.5 hours or until desired doneness.

Nutrient Value: *Energy:* 460, *Fat:* 32g, *Protein:* 36g, *Carbs:* 1g, *Fiber:* 0g

BBQ Brisket Pizza

Prep Duration: 20 mins

Cooking: 15 mins

Yield: 4

Materials:

- 1 lb. beef brisket, cooked and shredded
- 1 pizza dough
- 1/2 cup BBQ sauce
- 1 cup moz.zarella cheese
- 1 red onion, thinly sliced

Method

1. Spread BBQ sauce on pizza dough.
2. Top with cheese, brisket, and onion.
3. Bake in a 475°F (245°C) about for 15 mins.

Nutrient Value: *Energy:* 540, *Fat:* 22g, *Protein:* 32g, *Carbs:* 50g, *Fiber:* 2g

Garlic Butter Roast Chicken

Prep Duration: 20 mins

Cooking: 1.5 hours

Yield: 6

Materials:

- 4 lb. whole chicken
- 4 garlic cloves, minced
- 1/4 cup butter, softened
- Salt and pepper

Method

1. Mix butter with garlic.
2. Rub over and under chicken skin.
3. Roast using a 375°F (190°C) oven for 1.5 hours or till juices run clear.

Nutrient Value: *Energy:* 440, *Fat:* 28g, *Protein:* 40g, *Carbs:* 1g, *Fiber:* 0g

Teriyaki Ribs

Prep Duration: 20 mins

Cooking: 2.5 hours

Yield: 4

Materials:

- 2 lb. pork ribs
- 1/2 cup teriyaki sauce
- 1/4 cup honey
- 1 tbsp sesame seeds

Method

1. Mix teriyaki sauce and honey.
2. Glaze ribs with the mixture.
3. Bake in a 275°F (135°C) oven for 2.5 hours.
4. Sprinkle with sesame seeds.

Nutrient Value: *Energy:* 610, *Fat:* 34g, *Protein:* 48g, *Carbs:* 34g, *Fiber:* 0g

Brisket Tacos

Prep Duration: 20 mins

Cooking: 3 hours

Yield: 6

Materials:

- 2 lb. beef brisket, cooked and shredded
- 12 small tortillas
- 1 cup pico de gallo
- 1/2 cup sour cream
- Salt and pepper

Method

1. Warm brisket in a skillet.
2. Serve on tortillas with pico de gallo and sour cream.

Nutrient Value: *Energy:* 430, *Fat:* 20g, *Protein:* 28g, *Carbs:* 35g, *Fiber:* 3g

Sunday Roast with Vegetables

Prep Duration: 30 mins

Cooking: 2 hours

Yield: 6

Materials:

- 3 lb. beef roast
- 3 carrots, chopped
- 3 potatoes, quartered
- 2 onions, quartered
- Salt and pepper

Method

1. Season beef and place in a roasting pan.
2. Surround with vegetables.
3. Roast using a 375°F (190°C) oven for 2 hours.

Nutrient Value: *Energy:* 460, *Fat:* 20g, *Protein:* 40g, *Carbs:* 30g, *Fiber:* 5g

Spiced Ribs with Cumin and Coriander

Prep Duration: 15 mins

Cooking: 3 hours

Yield: 4

Materials:

- 2 lb. pork ribs
- 2 tsp cumin
- 2 tsp coriander
- 1 tsp paprika
- Salt and pepper

Method

1. Season ribs with spices.
2. Bake in a 275°F (135°C) oven for 3 hours.

Nutrient Value: *Energy:* 590, *Fat:* 34g, *Protein:* 50g, *Carbs:* 2g, *Fiber:* 1g

SEAFOOD SPECIALTIES: SALMON, SARDINES, MACKEREL

Honey Glazed Salmon

Prep Duration: 10 mins

Cooking: 15 mins

Yield: 4

Materials:

- 4 salmon fillets
- 3 tbsp honey
- 2 tbsp soy sauce
- 1 garlic clove, minced
- Salt and pepper

Method

1. Mix honey, soy sauce, and garlic.
2. Season salmon with salt and pepper.
3. Glaze salmon with mixture.
4. Bake for 15 mins at 400°F.

Nutrient Value: *Energy:* 320, *Fat:* 14g, *Protein:* 34g, *Carbs:* 14g, *Fiber:* 0g

Grilled Sardines with Lemon Herb Butter

Prep Duration: 15 mins

Cooking: 10 mins

Yield: 4

Materials:

- 12 fresh sardines
- 4 tbsp butter, softened
- 1 lemon, zest and juice
- 2 tbsp parsley, chopped
- Salt and pepper

Method

1. Combine butter, lemon zest, juice, and parsley.
2. Add seasonings on sardines.
3. Grill sardines for 5 mins on both side.
4. Serve with lemon herb butter.

Nutrient Value: *Energy:* 220, *Fat:* 15g, *Protein:* 19g, *Carbs:* 2g, *Fiber:* 0g

Mackerel with Tomato and Capers

Prep Duration: 10 mins

Cooking: 20 mins

Yield: 4

Materials:

- 4 mackerel fillets
- 2 tomatoes, sliced
- 2 tbsp capers

- 1 tbsp olive oil
- Salt and pepper

Method

1. Add seasonings in the mackerel.
2. Warm the boil in a pan to cook mackerel for 5 mins each side.
3. Put in tomatoes and capers, cook for another 10 mins.

Nutrient Value: *Energy:* 230, *Fat:* 12g, *Protein:* 25g, *Carbs:* 4g, *Fiber:* 1g

Salmon Patties with Dill Sauce

Prep Duration: 20 mins
Cooking: 15 mins
Yield: 4

Materials:

- 2 cups salmon, cooked and flaked
- 1 egg
- 1/2 cup breadcrumbs
- 1/4 cup mayonnaise
- 1 tbsp dill
- 1 tbsp lemon juice
- Salt and pepper

Method

1. Mix salmon, egg, breadcrumbs, salt, and pepper.
2. Shape them in patties.
3. Cook in a skillet for 7 mins each side.
4. Mix mayonnaise, dill, and lemon juice for sauce.

5. Serve patties with sauce.

Nutrient Value: *Energy:* 300, *Fat:* 15g, *Protein:* 28g, *Carbs:* 12g, *Fiber:* 1g

Sardine and Tomato Pasta

Prep Duration: 10 mins
Cooking: 20 mins
Yield: 4

Materials:

- 8 oz. spaghetti
- 1 can sardines in oil
- 1 can (15 oz.) diced tomatoes
- 2 garlic cloves, minced
- 1/4 cup parsley, chopped
- Salt and pepper

Method

1. Cook spaghetti.
2. In a pan, sauté garlic, put in tomatoes with sardines.
3. Cook for 10 mins.
4. Mix with spaghetti, add parsley, salt, and pepper.

Nutrient Value: *Energy:* 320, *Fat:* 8g, *Protein:* 18g, *Carbs:* 44g, *Fiber:* 3g

Mackerel Salad with Mustard Dressing

Prep Duration: 15 mins

Cooking: 0 mins

Yield: 4

Materials:

- 2 mackerel fillets, cooked and flaked
- 6 cups mixed salad greens
- 1/4 cup mustard
- 2 tbsp honey
- 2 tbsp vinegar
- Salt and pepper

Method

1. Mix mustard, vinegar, pepper, honey, and pepper for dressing.
2. Put in mackerel and greens in dressing.

Nutrient Value: *Energy:* 170, *Fat:* 6g, *Protein:* 17g, *Carbs:* 12g, *Fiber:* 2g

Salmon and Asparagus Foil Packets

Prep Duration: 15 mins

Cooking: 25 mins

Yield: 4

Materials:

- 4 salmon fillets
- 1 bunch asparagus, trimmed
- 2 tbsp olive oil
- 2 tbsp lemon juice
- Salt and pepper

Method

1. Place salmon along with asparagus on foil.
2. Top with oil and lemon juice.
3. Add the seasonings.
4. Seal foil and bake for 25 mins at 375°F.

Nutrient Value: *Energy:* 310, *Fat:* 16g, *Protein:* 34g, *Carbs:* 4g, *Fiber:* 2g

Sardine Toast with Avocado

Prep Duration: 10 mins

Cooking: 5 mins

Yield: 4

Materials:

- 1 can sardines in oil
- 2 avocados, mashed
- 4 slices of whole-grain toast
- 1 tbsp lemon juice
- Salt and pepper

Method

1. Mash avocados with lemon juice, salt, and pepper.
2. Spread on toast.
3. Top with sardines.

Nutrient Value: *Energy:* 280, *Fat:* 16g, *Protein:* 12g, *Carbs:* 25g, *Fiber:* 8g

Mackerel and Potato Hash

Prep Duration: 15 mins

Cooking: 30 mins

Yield: 4

Materials:

- 2 mackerel fillets, cooked and flaked
- 2 potatoes, diced
- 1 onion, chopped
- 2 tbsp olive oil
- Salt and pepper

Method

1. Warm the oil in a pan.
2. Put in potatoes along with onion, cook till they turn brown.
3. Put in mackerel, salt, as well as pepper.
4. Cook for additional 10 mins.

Nutrient Value: *Energy:* 250, *Fat:* 10g, *Protein:* 15g, *Carbs:* 26g, *Fiber:* 3g

Salmon and Spinach Curry

Prep Duration: 15 mins

Cooking: 20 mins

Yield: 4

Materials:

- 4 salmon fillets
- 2 cups spinach
- 1 onion, chopped
- 2 tbsp curry paste
- 1 can (15 oz.) coconut milk
- 2 tbsp oil
- Salt

Method

1. Warm the oil in a pan.
2. Cook onion till translucent.
3. Add curry paste, coconut milk, along with salmon.
4. Simmer for 10 mins.
5. Put in spinach and salt.
6. Cook until wilted.

Nutrient Value: *Energy:* 430, *Fat:* 28g, *Protein:* 33g, *Carbs:* 10g, *Fiber:* 2g

Sardine and Lemon Pasta

Prep Duration: 10 mins

Cooking: 15 mins

Yield: 4

Materials:

- 8 oz. linguine
- 1 can sardines in oil
- 1 lemon, zest and juice
- 2 garlic cloves, minced
- 2 tbsp olive oil

Method

1. Cook linguine.
2. In a skillet, heat oil, cook garlic.
3. Add sardines, lemon zest, and juice.
4. Mix with linguine.

Nutrient Value: *Energy:* 330, *Fat:* 12g, *Protein:* 18g, *Carbs:* 38g, *Fiber:* 2g

Mackerel and Vegetable Stir-Fry

Prep Duration: 15 mins
Cooking: 15 mins
Yield: 4

Materials:

- 2 mackerel fillets, cooked and flaked
- 2 cups mixed vegetables (broccoli, bell pepper, carrot)
- 2 tbsp soy sauce
- 1 tbsp ginger, minced
- 2 tbsp oil

Method

1. Warm the oil in a pan.
2. Cook vegetables and ginger until tender.
3. Add mackerel and soy sauce.
4. Let it cook for 5 mins.

Nutrient Value: *Energy:* 220, *Fat:* 10g, *Protein:* 17g, *Carbs:* 15g, *Fiber:* 4g

Salmon Ceviche

Prep Duration: 20 mins
Cooking: 0 mins (Marinate for 2 hours)
Yield: 4

Materials:

- 2 salmon fillets, diced

- 1 lime, juice
- 1/2 red onion, thinly sliced
- 1 chili, chopped
- 1 tbsp cilantro, chopped
- Salt

Method

1. Mix salmon, lime juice, onion, chili, cilantro, and salt.
2. Refrigerate for 2 hours before serving.

Nutrient Value: *Energy:* 200, *Fat:* 8g, *Protein:* 25g, *Carbs:* 7g, *Fiber:* 1g

Sardine Salad with Olives

Prep Duration: 15 mins
Cooking: 0 mins
Yield: 4

Materials:

- 1 can sardines in oil
- 2 cups mixed greens
- 1/2 cup olives
- 1/4 cup feta cheese
- 2 tbsp balsamic vinegar
- Salt and pepper

Method

1. Toss sardines, greens, olives, feta, balsamic vinegar, salt, and pepper.

Nutrient Value: *Energy:* 220, *Fat:* 15g, *Protein:* 12g, *Carbs:* 8g, *Fiber:* 2g

Mackerel on Rye with Pickled Onions

Prep Duration: 20 mins

Cooking: 0 mins

Yield: 4

Materials:

- 2 mackerel fillets, cooked and flaked
- 4 slices rye bread
- 1 red onion, thinly sliced
- 1/4 cup vinegar
- Salt

Method

1. Mix onion with vinegar and let sit for 15 mins.
2. Drain.
3. Place mackerel on rye bread and top with pickled onions.

Nutrient Value: *Energy:* 240, *Fat:* 8g, *Protein:* 20g, *Carbs:* 24g, *Fiber:* 4g

EXOTIC MEATS: BISON, VENISON, OSTRICH

Grilled Bison Burgers

Prep Duration: 15 mins

Cooking: 10 mins

Yield: 4

Materials:

- 1 lb. ground bison
- 4 hamburger buns
- 1 onion, sliced
- 4 lettuce leaves
- Salt and pepper

Method

1. Season bison using the seasonings.
2. Form into patties.
3. Grill boyh sides for 5 mins.
4. Serve on buns with onion and lettuce.

Nutrient Value: *Energy:* 280, *Fat:* 11g, *Protein:* 29g, *Carbs:* 20g, *Fiber:* 2g

Venison Stew

Prep Duration: 20 mins

Cooking: 2 hours

Yield: 6

Materials:

- 2 lb. venison, cubed
- 3 carrots, chopped
- 3 potatoes, diced
- 1 onion, chopped
- 4 cups beef broth
- Salt and pepper

Method

1. Brown venison in a pot.
2. Add vegetables and broth.
3. Simmer for 2 hours.
4. Add the seasonings.

Nutrient Value: *Energy:* 330, *Fat:* 8g, *Protein:* 40g, *Carbs:* 30g, *Fiber:* 4g

Ostrich Steak with Chimichurri

Prep Duration: 20 mins

Cooking: 15 mins

Yield: 4

Materials:

- 4 ostrich steaks
- 1/4 cup parsley, chopped
- 2 garlic cloves, minced
- 2 tbsp vinegar
- 1/4 cup olive oil
- Salt and pepper

Method

1. Season the steaks.
2. Grill each side for 7 mins.
3. Combine oil, garlic, parsley and vinegar for chimichurri.
4. Serve steaks with sauce.

Nutrient Value: *Energy:* 290, *Fat:* 15g, *Protein:* 30g, *Carbs:* 2g, *Fiber:* 1g

Bison Meatballs with Tomato Sauce

Prep Duration: 25 mins
Cooking: 30 mins
Yield: 4

Materials:

- 1 lb. ground bison
- 1 can (15 oz.) crushed tomatoes
- 1 garlic clove, minced
- 1/4 cup breadcrumbs
- 1 egg
- Salt and pepper

Method

1. Mix egg, breadcrumbs, salt, bison, and pepper.
2. Shape into meatballs.
3. Cook in a pan.
4. Add garlic and tomatoes.
5. Simmer for 20 mins.

Nutrient Value: *Energy:* 310, *Fat:* 12g, *Protein:* 30g, *Carbs:* 20g, *Fiber:* 3g

Venison and Mushroom Pie

Prep Duration: 30 mins
Cooking: 45 mins
Yield: 6

Materials:

- 1 lb. venison, cubed
- 1 cup mushrooms, sliced
- 1 onion, chopped
- 2 cups beef broth
- 1 pie crust
- Salt and pepper

Method

1. Cook venison, mushrooms, and onion in a pot.
2. Put in the broth and let it simmer for 20 mins.
3. Pour into a pie dish.
4. Cover with crust.
5. Bake for 25 mins at 375°F.

Nutrient Value: *Energy:* 390, *Fat:* 18g, *Protein:* 30g, *Carbs:* 30g, *Fiber:* 2g

Ostrich and Vegetable Stir-Fry

Prep Duration: 20 mins
Cooking: 15 mins
Yield: 4

Materials:

- 1 lb. ostrich, thinly sliced

- 2 cups mixed vegetables (bell peppers, broccoli, snap peas)
- 2 tbsp soy sauce
- 1 tbsp ginger, minced
- 2 tbsp oil

Method

1. Warm the oil in a pan.
2. Cook ostrich till browned.
3. Put in vegetables, ginger, along with soy sauce.
4. Cook till vegetables are soft.

Nutrient Value: *Energy:* 230, *Fat:* 9g, *Protein:* 27g, *Carbs:* 10g, *Fiber:* 3g

Bison Chili

Prep Duration: 20 mins
Cooking: 1.5 hours
Yield: 6

Materials:

- 1 lb. ground bison
- 1 can (15 oz.) kidney beans
- 1 can (15 oz.) diced tomatoes
- 1 onion, chopped
- 2 tbsp chili powder
- Salt and pepper

Method

1. Brown bison and onion in a pot.
2. Put in the beans,, chili powder, pepper, tomatoes, and salt.
3. Let it simmer for 1.5 hours.

Nutrient Value: *Energy:* 310, *Fat:* 10g, *Protein:* 25g, *Carbs:* 30g, *Fiber:* 8g

Venison Sausages with Caramelized Onions

Prep Duration: 15 mins
Cooking: 25 mins
Yield: 4

Materials:

- 8 venison sausages
- 2 onions, thinly sliced
- 2 tbsp brown sugar
- 2 tbsp balsamic vinegar
- 1 tbsp oil

Method

1. Cook sausages in a skillet.
2. In another skillet, warm the oil and cook onions till soft.
3. Put in sugar along with vinegar.
4. Cook until caramelized.
5. Serve sausages with onions.

Nutrient Value: *Energy:* 320, *Fat:* 14g, *Protein:* 26g, *Carbs:* 22g, *Fiber:* 2g

Grilled Ostrich with Garlic Herb Butter

Prep Duration: 20 mins

Cooking: 15 mins

Yield: 4

Materials:

- 4 ostrich steaks
- 4 tbsp butter, softened
- 2 garlic cloves, minced
- 2 tbsp parsley, chopped
- Salt and pepper

Method

1. Season the steaks.
2. Grill on both sides for 7 mins each.
3. Combine butter, garlic, and parsley.
4. Top steaks with butter mixture.

Nutrient Value: *Energy:* 300, *Fat:* 16g, *Protein:* 30g, *Carbs:* 2g, *Fiber:* 0g

Bison Tacos with Salsa Verde

Prep Duration: 20 mins

Cooking: 10 mins

Yield: 4

Materials:

- 1 lb. ground bison
- 8 small tortillas
- 1 cup salsa verde
- 1/4 cup cilantro, chopped
- Salt and pepper

Method

1. Cook bison in a skillet.
2. Season with salt and pepper.
3. Serve on tortillas with salsa verde and cilantro.

Nutrient Value: *Energy:* 330, *Fat:* 12g, *Protein:* 25g, *Carbs:* 30g, *Fiber:* 3g

Venison Curry

Prep Duration: 20 mins

Cooking: 45 mins

Yield: 6

Materials:

- 2 lb. venison, cubed
- 2 tbsp curry paste
- 1 can (15 oz.) coconut milk
- 1 onion, chopped
- Salt and pepper

Method

1. Brown venison and onion in a pot.
2. Put in the curry paste and coconut milk.
3. Simmer for 45 mins.
4. Add the seasonings.

Nutrient Value: *Energy:* 340, *Fat:* 14g, *Protein:* 40g, *Carbs:* 10g, *Fiber:* 1g

Ostrich Meatballs in Tomato Sauce

Prep Duration: 25 mins

Cooking: 30 mins

Yield: 4

Materials:

- 1 lb. ground ostrich
- 1 can (15 oz.) crushed tomatoes
- 1 egg
- 1/4 cup breadcrumbs
- 2 garlic cloves, minced
- Salt and pepper

Method

1. Mix ostrich, salt, breadcrumbs, egg, and pepper.
2. Shape them in meatballs.
3. Cook in a pan.
4. Add garlic and tomatoes.
5. Simmer for 20 mins.

Nutrient Value: *Energy:* 260, *Fat:* 9g, *Protein:* 25g, *Carbs:* 20g, *Fiber:* 3g

Grilled Bison Steaks with Chimichurri

Prep Duration: 20 mins

Cooking: 15 mins

Yield: 4

Materials:

- 4 bison steaks
- 1/4 cup parsley, chopped
- 2 garlic cloves, minced
- 2 tbsp vinegar
- 1/4 cup olive oil
- Salt and pepper

Method

1. Season the steaks.
2. Grill each side for 7 mins.
3. Combine parsley, garlic, vinegar, and oil for chimichurri.
4. Serve steaks with sauce.

Nutrient Value: *Energy:* 310, *Fat:* 16g, *Protein:* 30g, *Carbs:* 2g, *Fiber:* 1g

Venison and Blueberry Sausages

Prep Duration: 25 mins

Cooking: 15 mins

Yield: 4

Materials:

- 1 lb. ground venison
- 1/2 cup blueberries
- 2 garlic cloves, minced
- Salt and pepper

Method

1. Mix venison, blueberries, garlic, salt, and pepper.
2. Shape them in sausages.
3. Cook in a pan for 15 mins.

Nutrient Value: *Energy:* 220, *Fat:* 8g, *Protein:* 28g, *Carbs:* 8g, *Fiber:* 1g

Ostrich Skewers with Pineapple and Bell Peppers

Prep Duration: 20 mins

Cooking: 15 mins

Yield: 4

Materials:

- 1 lb. ostrich, cubed
- 1 cup pineapple, cubed
- 1 bell pepper, cubed
- 2 tbsp soy sauce
- 1 tbsp honey

Method

1. Skewer ostrich, pineapple, and bell pepper.
2. Mix soy sauce and honey.
3. Brush skewers with mixture.
4. Grill for 15 mins.

Nutrient Value: *Energy:* 220, *Fat:* 4g, *Protein:* 30g, *Carbs:* 20g, *Fiber:* 2g

SUPPLEMENTS & HYDRATION

The question of supplementing is one of the most frequent when starting a carnivorous diet. In the end, worries about conceivable nutrient deficiencies are understandable when one shuns the diverse range of plant-based diets. On the other hand, can meat alone supply all the nutrients needed for a carnivore diet, or do supplements need to be taken as well?

Our predecessors historically thrived on diets that were primarily reliant on animal sources, especially during particular seasons or in particular places where plant resources were in short supply. This implies that the majority, if not all, of the necessary nutrients might be obtained through a well-planned carnivore diet. As an illustration, organ meats are richly stocked with an array of minerals and vitamins and are frequently referred to as nature's multivitamins. With high levels of vitamin A, B vitamins, iron, and copper, the liver is a single-organ powerhouse of nutrition.

However, other vitamins, such as vitamin C, which are prevalent in plant diets are far less prevalent in animal products. The good news is that the quantity of vitamin C needed by the body may decrease on a low-carbohydrate diet and that the little amounts available in organ meats like liver may be adequate. Similar to omega-6 fatty acids, omega-3 fatty acids are present in fatty fish and pasture-grown meats but may need specific attention, especially if one's diet includes a lot of conventionally raised meats, which can have a greater omega-6 fatty acid content. Another thing to think about is your intake of electrolytes, especially when switching over to a carnivorous diet.

The so-called "keto flu" or "carnivore flu," which affects some people and is characterized by symptoms including weariness, headaches, and cramps in the muscles, can occur. The main cause of this is usually a quick loss of electrolytes like sodium, potassium, and magnesium. Even though nutrients can be obtained from meat, particularly from bone broths, some people find it helpful to supplement, at least temporarily.

The unique diversity of each person is another aspect that can require supplements. Nutrient needs can change as a result of genetics, medical problems, or certain physiological needs, such as pregnancy. According to blood tests and medical advice, customized supplementation may be helpful in certain situations.

In conclusion, while a well-rounded carnivore diet with an emphasis on the intake of the entire animal can cover the majority of nutritional demands, supplements can play a role in addressing particular problems or individual requirements. With the understanding that more isn't necessarily better, it's critical to approach dietary supplements with discernment. The need for and appropriateness of supplements must be determined by regular health examinations, discussions with medical specialists, and body awareness.

Importance of staying hydrated and the role of electrolytes

Approximately 60% of the human body is made up of water, which is essential to all physiological processes and is the basis of life. It is crucial to stay hydrated for a variety of reasons, including temperature regulation and digestive support. Understanding hydration and the related function of electrolytes becomes even more important when implementing dietary changes, such as the carnivore diet.

Water is essential for all cells, tissues, and organs to operate properly, therefore hydration goes beyond simply soothing thirst. Drinking enough water helps with joint lubrication, waste elimination, and the delivery of nutrients. Additionally, it influences mood and cognitive processes. Dehydration can cause headaches, weariness, and even a minor loss of coordination.

Hydration has unique intricacies within the setting of the carnivorous diet. The body naturally excretes more water as carbohydrate intake is reduced. This is so that the carbohydrates, particularly the glycogen that is stored in the muscles and liver, can hold the water. The water that is bound to glycogen is expelled as glycogen stores become depleted. In addition to emphasizing the need for greater fluid consumption, this may cause an initial weight reduction that is primarily due to water weight. Water is important, but electrolytes play a crucial role in maintaining hydration as well.

The balance of fluids flowing into and out of cells, tissues, and organs is crucially regulated by electrolytes, minerals that carry an electric charge. Key electrolytes that impact nerve impulses, muscular contractions, and pH equilibrium include sodium, potassium, magnesium, and calcium.

Electrolyte levels may become unbalanced on a carnivorous diet as a result of the alteration in water dynamics and modifications in food sources. Muscle cramps, lightheadedness, and irregular pulse are some of the signs of this imbalance, sometimes known as "Keto flu" or "carnivore flu." It's crucial to guarantee an appropriate intake of these minerals to combat this. Potassium and magnesium are abundant in bone broths, for instance.

On a carnivore diet, sodium is crucial and can be modified based on personal needs. It frequently has a poor rap about manufactured foods. Hydration can come from a variety of sources. While drinking plain water is always a good idea, adding broths or waters rich in minerals can help you stay hydrated and get the minerals your body needs. To facilitate a more seamless transition, some people also take electrolyte supplements, especially in the beginning stages of the diet.

The underlying importance of being hydrated and maintaining electrolyte balance is underscored by the carnivore diet, as with any dietary strategy, in conclusion. It serves as a reminder that, despite our attention being drawn to macronutrients like proteins and fats, the importance of the fundamentals, such as water and minerals, cannot be overstated. One can travel the carnivorous path with vigor and vitality by being proactive and mindful of their hydration needs.

CONCLUSION

Choosing to follow a carnivorous diet is more than simply a gourmet experience; it's also a deep investigation into human nutrition, evolutionary history, and personal well-being. A comprehensive picture has emerged as a result of our exploration of this diet's many facets, including its historical foundations, the science underlying its health benefits, the nuances of hydration, and the complexities of meat preparation.

The carnivore diet has layers of intricacy underneath its ostensibly simple meat-centric approach. The potential of the diet for holistic nutrition is highlighted by the significance of obtaining various meat types, notably nutrient-rich organ meats. Similarly how the emphasis on cooking Instructions highlights the diversity and richness that meat, in all of its forms, provides to the table, is another example of how cooking Instructions are important.

The diet does, however, present difficulties and matters to think about. A balanced and healthy journey as a carnivore depends on addressing potential traps, dispelling myths, and comprehending the subtleties of supplements and hydration. To create a satisfying carnivore experience, each element—from the importance of key flavors to the subtleties of meat preservation and safety — must be taken into consideration. In short, eating meat and other animal products isn't the only component of the carnivorous diet.

The goal is to improve our health, re-establish a connection to our ancestors' nutritional knowledge, and comprehend and respect the source of our food. The carnivore road can result in a lively convergence of flavor, health, and well-being if knowledge serves as our compass and mindfulness as our compass.

EXTRA CONTENT FOR OUR READERS

A Burst of Thanks and a Special Gift Just for You!

Hello dear Reader,

If you're reading these words, it means you've joined our marvelous community, and we couldn't be happier to have you!

✹ Your Opinion is Golden to Us! ✹

Your experience, thoughts, and emotions about the book in your hands are invaluable. We would be over the moon if you could **share your experience with our work on Amazon**. Whether you adored a specific recipe, found a tip particularly useful, or just enjoyed the journey through the pages, your sharing is a shining beacon for other readers and a fountain of inspiration for us authors.

❀ Your Exclusive BONUS Awaits! ❀

As a sign of our endless gratitude, we have prepared a special gift just for you. Not only will you have access to your current copy of the book in an exclusive digital color edition, further enriching your visual and culinary experience, but we've also reserved an additional gift for you.

"THE SUPERFOOD CODE: Explore Time-Tested Foods and Empower Your Health" is your extra ticket to a food discovery adventure, offering you a deep dive into the superfoods that have nourished and enriched generations, thanks to the secrets and practices revealed in the book.

🔥 Your Grilling Adventure Begins NOW! 🔥

Your culinary journey with us is just heating up! In addition to your exclusive bonuses, we're thrilled to also present you with a sizzling surprise: **"PIT BOSS GRILLING"**. This isn't merely a book - it's your ticket to becoming a master of the grill, transforming every barbecue into an unforgettable feast. From smoky, savory delights to tantalizingly sweet treats, you're about to explore the boundless world of flavors, all from the comfort of your own backyard. Get ready to uplift your grilling skills, surprise your loved ones with newfound culinary prowess, and embark on countless food adventures with the trusty Pit Boss by your side. Unlock secrets to crafting mouthwatering dishes that will not only satisfy your taste buds but also ignite a flame of excitement in every bite. Your journey through the enchanted world of grilling starts now, and we're thrilled to be joining you every step of the way!

✨ No Strings, Just Pure Enrichment ✨

Below you'll find an exclusive **QR CODE** that will guide you directly to your gift, ready to be downloaded and enjoyed, without any worry about subscribing to mailing lists or providing personal data. It's our simple, sincere gift to you.

We wish every moment you spend in the kitchen to be a delicious adventure and every meal to nourish both your body and soul.

With endless gratitude and warmth beyond words,

Michelle Burns

author.author1001@gmail.com

THANK YOU!

Made in the USA
Monee, IL
25 October 2023

45199223R00052